T0354697

Artificial Intelligence Theory For Management

Artificial Intelligence Theory For Management

Harry Katzan Jr.

iUniverse

ARTIFICIAL INTELLIGENCE THEORY
FOR MANAGEMENT

iUniverse books may be ordered through booksellers or by contacting:

iUniverse
1663 Liberty Drive
Bloomington, IN 47403
www.iuniverse.com
844-349-9409

ISBN: 978-1-6632-5615-7 (sc)
ISBN: 978-1-6632-5617-1 (hc)
ISBN: 978-1-6632-5616-4 (e)

Library of Congress Control Number: 2023917284

Print information available on the last page.

iUniverse rev. date: 09/08/2023

For Margaret, with all my love
now and forever

Introduction

This is an introductory book about Artificial Intelligence Theory. It is not for AI specialists. It is too simple for them. As unusual as it sounds, there is a very good reason for its existence. There are existing books on the subject that are very good but are very difficult to read. It's that simple. The concepts are complicated and some require complex math. A typical example is the subject of neural networks. The book uses Service Science as the presentation mechanism since artificial intelligence theory using ontology is not exactly floating around in cyberspace. After all, artificial intelligence is essentially a service to start with.

A manager should know what theory governs the new field of artificial intelligence, because he or she will be involved if only at the listening level or going into a meeting. Artificial Intelligence is here to stay this time. It's a third try to bring the subject to the forefront. It is here for the future, and it is here to stay because the world needs it. We are in the midst of war, preparation for defense, a dismal economic outlook, crime, killing, and so forth. We need it because if we continue the way we are going, we won't be going anywhere for very long. Practically everything is disarray. Just name them: violence, shady politics, global warming, discrimination, abortion, women's birth problems, men's cancer. What is the solution? It is twofold. Equitably use the information we have and permit the human race to communicate and act in a reasonable manner. Through Artificial Intelligence, often

referred to as AI, we have the key to managing our lives on a daily basis – worldwide.

There is a lot going on in the area of AI, as it's called. Young people all over the place are into it. New software is being developed. There is a generative AI system named ChatGPT developed by a company named *OpenAI* that has done a good job with new developments. What is a manager to do.

A company named IBM is in the field with a system called IBM Watson, that operates out of the cloud is also in the game. In fact, this book can give you some insight into what is going on. It contains three snippets on ChatGPT, IBM Watson, and Data Science that are included at the end of the book.

Instead of business and government leaders having to tell us what they are going to do, we can and will be addressing that subject through AI.

AI is a systems concept, not a single piece of software you can buy at a local store. Can you imagine a kid telling you they have computers and AI, meaning software apps. You will be able to obtain AI capability but it needs to be blended into the infrastructure to its host organization. A good example is the Watson System developed by IBM. It can, will, and has done wonders with design and analytics, but you probably will need some help in employing the computational infrastructure. There are already competition systems but Watson is mentioned because it beat some Jeopardy! champions at their own game.

So, here is what we are providing to you with in this book. A straightforward description of the subject of AI that is easy to read. No more and no less. You can jump into this book at any point and get something out of it. In addition, you will get a quick survey of Service Science. After all, Artificial Intelligence is a service

In the best sense of the word.

The book is not expensive and something you would enjoy giving to a relative or friend. The book adheres to the author's principle of no sex, no violence, and no bad language. It is accessible to all readers. This need not be said for a book of this type, but I like saying it.

Enjoy the book if you can, You will be pleased, if you only read parts of the book.

The Author

Contents

PART I

Artificial Intelligence

The Basics

Artificial Intelligence is commonly regarded as the science of making machines do things that would require intelligence if performed by humans. Everyone knows this, but it must be mentioned anyway. In addition to being a rather trite definition, the foregoing remark is additionally not intellectually useful. For example, the task of computing the payroll would require human intelligence if done by hand but is regarded as commonplace data processing application. Of course, payroll is not a trivial application and neither are inventory management, online banking, and numerical computing - to name only a few cases. Well then, what characterizes an AI application? Moreover, is there a well-defined dividing line between AI and non-AI? The questions are largely rhetorical since it really doesn't really matter how a particular application is classed. Artificial Intelligence, known as AI, a pragmatic discipline, is characterized more as a way of doing things than a specific well-defined technical concept.

The AI Approach

It is possible to approach Artificial Intelligence from two points of view. Both approaches make use of programs and programming techniques. The first approach is to investigate the general principles of intelligence. The second is to study human thought, in particular.

1

Those persons engaged in the investigation of the principles of intelligence are normally charged with the development of systems that appear to be intelligent. This activity is commonly regarded as "artificial intelligence," which incorporates both engineering and computer science components.

Those persons engaged in the study of human thought attempt to emulate human mental processes to a lesser or greater degree. This activity can be regarded as a form of "computer simulation," such that the elements of a relevant psychological theory are represented in a computer program. The objective of this approach is to generate psychological theories of human thought. The discipline is generally known as "Cognitive Science."

In reality, the differences between artificial intelligence and cognitive science tend to vary between "not so much" and "quite a lot" - depending upon the complexity of the underlying task. Most applications, as a matter of fact, contain elements from both approaches.

The Scope of AI

It is possible to zoom in on the scope of AI by focusing on the processes involved. At one extreme, the concentration is on the practicalities of doing AI programming, with an emphasis on symbolic programming languages and AI machines. In this context, AI can be regarded as a new way of doing programming. It necessarily follows that hardware/software systems with AI components have the potential for enhanced end-user effectiveness,

At the other extreme, AI could be regarded as the study of intelligent computation. This is a more grandiose and encompassing focus with the objective of building a systematic and encompassing focus with the objective of building a systematic theory of intellectual processes - regardless if they model human thought or not.

It would appear, therefore, that AI is more concerned with intelligence in general and less involved with human thought in particular. Thus, it may be contended that humans and computers are simply two options in the genus of information processing systems.

The Modern Era of Artificial Intelligence

The modern era of artificial intelligence effectively began with the summer conference at Dartmouth College in Hanover, New Hampshire in 1956. The key participants were Shannon from Bell Labs, Minsky from Harvard (later M.I.T.), McCarthy from Dartmouth (later M.I.T. and Stanford), and Simon from Carnegie Tech (renamed Carnegie Mellon). The key results from the conference were twofold:

- It legitimized the notion of AI and brought together a raft of piecemeal research activities.
- The name "Artificial Intelligence" was coined and the name more than anything else has had a profound influence on the future direction of artificial intelligence.

The stars of the conference were Simon, and his associate Allen Newell, who demonstrated the Logic Theorist - the first well-known reasoning program. They preferred the name, "Complex Information Processing," for the new fledging science of the artificial. In the end, Shannon and McCarthy won out with the zippy and provocative name, "artificial intelligence." In all probability, the resulting controversy surrounding the name artificial intelligence served to sustain a certain critical mass of academic interest in the subject - even during periods of sporadic activity and questionable results.

One of the disadvantages of the pioneering AI conference was the simple fact that an elite group of scientists was created that would effectively decide "what AI is and what AI isn't," and how to best achieve it. The end result was that AI became closely aligned with psychology and not with neurophysiology and to a lesser degree with electrical engineering. AI became a software science with the main objective of producing intelligent artifacts. In short, it became a closed group, and this effectively constrained the field to a large degree.

In recent years, the direction of AI research has been altered somewhat by an apparent relationship with brain research and cognitive technology, which is known as the design of joint human-machine cognitive systems. Two obvious fallouts of the new direction are the well-known "Connection Machine," and the computer vision projects at the National Bureau of Standards in the United States. That information is somewhat out of date,

but the history gives some insight into what AI is today and where it will be heading.

Early Work on the Concept of Artificial Intelligence

The history of AI essentially goes back to the philosophy of Plato, who wrote that. "All knowledge must be able to be stated in explicit definitions which anyone could apply," thereby eliminating appeals to judgment and intuition. Plato's student Aristotle continued in this noble tradition in the development of the categorical syllogism, which plays an important part in modern logic.

The mathematician Leibnitz attempted to quantify all knowledge and reasoning through an exact algebraic system by which all objects are assigned a unique characteristic number. Using these characteristic numbers, therefore, rules for the combination of problems would be establishes and controversies could be resolved by calculation.

The underlying philosophical idea was conceptually simple: Reduce the whole of human knowledge into a single formal system. The notion of formal representation has become the basis of AI and cognitive science theories since it involves the reduction of the totality of human experience to a set of basic elements that can be glued together in various ways.

To sum up, the philosophical phenomenologists argue that it impossible to subject pure phenomena - i.e., mental acts which give meaning to the world - to formal analysis. Of course, AI people do not agree. They contend that "there is no ghost in the machine," and this is meant to imply that intelligence is a set of well-defined physical processes.

The discussion is reminiscent of the mind/brain controversy and it appears that the AI perspective is that "the mind is what the brain does." Of course, the phenomenologists would reply that the definition of mind exists beyond the physical neurons; it also incorporates the intangible concepts of what the neurons do.

Accordingly, strong AI is defined in the literature as the case wherein an appropriately programmed computer actually is a "mind." Weak AI, on the other hand is the emulation of human intelligence, as we know it.

Intelligence and Intelligent Systems

There seems to be some value in the ongoing debate over the intelligence of AI artifacts. The term "artificial" in artificial intelligence helps us out. One could therefore contend that intelligence is natural if it is biological and artificial otherwise. This conclusion skirts the controversy and frees intellectual energy for more purposeful activity.

The abstract notion of intelligence, therefore, is conceptualized, and natural and artificial intelligence serve as specific instances.

The subjects of understanding and learning could be treated in a similar manner. The productive tasks of identifying the salient aspects of intelligence, understanding, and learning emerge as the combined goal of AI and cognitive science. For example, the concepts of representation and reasoning, to name only two of many, have been studied productively from both artificial and biological viewpoints. Software products that are currently available can be evaluated in the basis of how well they can support the basic AI technologies,

The key question then becomes: How well do natural and artificial systems, as discussed above, match up to the abstract notion of intelligence

Cognitive Technology

Cognitive technology is the set of concepts and techniques for developing joint human-machine cognitive systems. People are obviously interested in cognitive systems because they are goal directed and employ self-knowledge of the environment to monitor, plan, and modify their actions in the pursuit of their goals. In a logical sense, joint human-machine systems can also be classed as being cognitive because of the availability of computational techniques for automating decisions and exercising operational control over physical processes and organizational activities.

Recent advances in heuristic techniques coupled with methods of knowledge representation and automated reasoning have made it possible to couple human cognitive systems with

artificial cognitive systems. Accordingly, joint systems in this case would necessarily have the following attributes:

- Be problem driven, rather than technology driven.
- Effective models of underlying processes are needed.
- Control of decision making processes must be shared between human and artificial components.

Clearly, cognitive technology represents a possible (if not probable) paradigm shift whereby the human self-view can and wake in the not-too-distant future.

Virtual Systems and Imagination

Methods for reasoning in expert and cognitive systems are well defined. Rules and representation effectively solve the problem. There appears to be a set of problems, however, that seem to evade such a simple solution as rules and representation.

A sophisticated model of a cognitive system must incorporate the capability of reasoning about itself or another cognitive system and about the computational facilities that provide the cognition. When a person, for example, is asked to reason about the feelings of the probable response of another person, a set of rules is normally invoked to provide the desired response. If no rule set exists, then a virtual process is engaged that proceeds somewhat as follows:

- The object process is imagined, i.e. you effectively put yourself in the other person's shoes, so to speak.

- The neural inputs are "faked" and the brain responds in somewhat the same manner as it would in real life.
- The result is observed exactly as though it had taken place.

Thus, a sort of simulation of a self-model is employed. This type of analysis might be invoked if someone were asked, for example, how they would feel if they had just received the news they had contracted an incurable disease.

The process, described above, is essentially what an operating system does while controlling the execution of a "guest" operating system. Inputs and outputs are interpreted, but machine code is actually executed.

It necessarily follows that executable models, as suggested here, are as much a form of knowledge as are rules and facts. But, Is It intelligent?

Exploring the issue even further, a sharp borderline between intelligent and non-intelligent behavior, in the abstract sense, probably does not exist. Nevertheless, some essential qualities might be the following:

- To respond to situations very flexibly.
- To take advantage of fortuitous circumstances.
- To make sense out of ambiguous or contradictory messages.
- To recognize the relative importance of different elements of a situation.

- To find similarities between situations despite differences which may separate them.
- To draw distinctions between situations despite similarities which may link them.
- To synthesize new concepts by taking old concepts and putting them together in new ways.
- To come up with ideas that the are novel.

Viewed in this manner, intelligence is a form of computation. Effective intelligence then is a process (perhaps a computer program) and an appropriate machine in which to execute the process.

Systems Concepts and AI

An interesting viewpoint the concerns the evolution of data processing has emerged from the AI business. The task of designing a rule base and an associate fact base is somewhat analogous to designing an information system. Moreover, both kinds of systems appear to evolve in a similar manner. For this analysis, it should be assumed that statements and computational processes (i.e., modules) are the same (or synonymous).

A sensory stimulation is associated with a statement. (Incidentally, this concept is known as associations, wherein a sensation is associated with an idea, and that idea leads to another idea, and so forth. This theory originated with Aristotle and was pursued by Hobbs, Locke, and Mill.). The associations reverberate through the system of statements, whereby a result is finally

achieved. The output can viewed as a prediction. Moreover, the system operates according to some form internal laws - such as the laws of mathematics.

When a prediction fails, continuing with the statement analogy, we question the validity of the set of statements. Revisions are normally in order. Since a direct correlation is usually possible between the stimuli and peripheral statements, these statements are preserved from revision. Other statements must bear the brunt of change. The other statements, however, can be regarded as the "frozen middle," since they result from internal laws. The end result that a priority judgment is necessary to change the peripheral statements and change the frozen middle. The priorities of course are in conflict and the preference commonly goes to the revision that disturbs the system the least.

Effectively, incremental changes are made to the system until a total revision is necessary - i.e., a rewrite of the internal including the Laws, the frozen middle, and the peripheral statements. As a total concept, major revisions serve to simplify a system. It necessarily follows that some attention should be given to systems evolution as a predictive technique.

Natural Systems

Developments in artificial intelligence have through the years tended to mirror natural systems. The two main targets in this area are natural language and vision. The field of connectionism is also introduced briefly. Locomotion and robotics are not included in the book.

Natural Language Processing

The use of language in an efficient and effective manner is considered to be an important aspect of human intelligence, and it is therefore no surprise that AI researchers have devoted a considerable amount of attention to the subject. Natural language is a complex area that had its roots in computer linguistics.

The subject of computational linguistics covers the computational mechanisms that form the basis of the use of natural language. The science is a discipline in is own right but lies on the periphery of artificial intelligence, philosophy, classical linguists and psychology. The goals of the field are:

- The investigation of human communications.
- The development of artificial systems with communications capability.

The goals of the field tend to work together. The scientific goal of understanding human language and its use allows us to better use the language and to facilitate the engineering goal to develop systems that process that language. The notion of science and engineering progressing in lock step is not unknown in modern society.

Natural language has evolved as a mechanism for communicating between human minds with all if their functional advantages and processing limitations. Accordingly, there is no underlying reason for computer systems that deal with natural language, or significant subsets of it, to process the language in the same manner that humans do. This is to be expected. Airplanes do not fly like birds, and clothes washers do not wash like people do.

Applications

The main areas of natural language processing are machine translation, document understanding, document generation, and natural language interaction. A fifth area that concerns word processing, word processing, desktop publishing, and electronic mail is also recognized but considered to be adjunct to this discussion.

Machine translation is concerned with the development of computational devices that read a document in one language and produce a document in another language. The ultimate goal is to perform the process in real time – as in a telephone conversation

between Japanese and English speaking persons, each speaking in their language. The science of machine translation is well developed and is applicable to specific domains of discourse — such as an owner's manual for an automobile.

The field has evolved through tree stages. The first step involved single word-by-word translation with a considerable amount of manual pre- and post- editing. The second stage recognized syntactic structure and progressed through a document on a sentence basis. In some cases, an intermediate language was used. In the third and current stage, preference semantics, contextual dependency, and other forms of semantic analyses are used to create a domain of discourse. Current results are very good for certain applications, such as technical reports and reference manuals. Machine translation probably will never do a good job on literature, because of the semantic structure normally associated with varying levels of meaning. A machine translation system can be used as a service facility in a comprehensive management system, and the domain of discourse will expand as technical writers learn to "write for translation."

In the field of professional translation, computer assisted translation (CAT) is currently the norm. Professional organizations, such as Berlitz, use a CAT system to build up a domain-specific vocabulary and can then expect excellent "automatic" translation results on associated projects. A typical application would be the machine translation of legal briefs related to a technical discipline, and a typical domain-specific vocabulary would be 17,000 words. One might conclude, therefore, that machine translation is and has

been a successful endeavor, provided that a reasonable definition of the term "success" is kept in mind.

Document Understanding

Document understanding is the process of abstracting the salient aspects of a document, which could range from a telex message to a business report. Clearly, similar techniques machine translation could be used. More specifically, typical applications of an "understanding machine" would be:

- Read and assimilate a document in order to be able to answer questions about it.
- Produce an abstract of a document for library-like purposes.
- Determine the relevant aspects if a document for directing it for further processing.
- Ascertain the salient aspects of a document to alert people that might be interested in it.

In some cases, such as in the processing of a telex message, a sophisticated analysis might not be necessary. For example, a simple content analysis, as in military intelligence or political science, coupled with a relevant profile for redirection is all that is necessary. On the other hand, the "deep structure" of a document could be needed for a question-answering system, where a full-blown semantic analysis would ordinarily be required.

Document generation refers to the process of translating information stored in a formal language into ordinary natural

language. Scientific, engineering, and technical artifacts are commonly stored in an internal form to facilitate processing, storage, and retrieval. Engineering drawings and repair procedures are two typical examples. The implication in the above discussion is that text is generated in the traditional form – i.e., printed or displayed on a video display unit. Generation of the spoken word is another option that has potential of the future. Clearly, this capability will be combined with reasoning systems to supply the user with detailed knowledge of how to resolve a particular situation as in the classical case of auto repair.

The primary use of natural language processing so far has been as an end-use interface component is a larger system, such as a database query system. The basic procedure operates somewhat as follows:

- The end user enters a query in natural language form.
- The request is scanned, parsed, and analyzed using natural language processing techniques.
- Ambiguities are resolved through interaction with the user.
- The natural language query facility constructs a query procedure.
- The query procedure is executed by the system.
- The results are returned to the user.

An analogous scheme can be used to control complex equipment and to supply expert advice (such as medical) to the front-end expert system

The modus operandi of natural language interface facilities are threefold:

- To generate executable query procedures, as covered above, that may be referred to as a "loosely coupled" interface to be used with database systems.
- To operate interpretively and generate queries internally from the interface system, and called a "closely coupled" interface to be used with control applications.
- To provide a "menu drive" language, whereby an end-user is supplied an option menu for generating the next word in a query.

The natural language processing process involves the use if a grammar and a lexicon together with a processor that associates input strings with an underlying structure. The grammar, which describes the allowable sentences in the language, and the lexicon, which is an inventory of the words in the universe of discourse and their inflectional, syntactic, and semantic properties, are the inputs to the processor along with the set of input strings. The processor operates through four components: a parser, a recognizer, an analyzer, and a transducer. The parser operates on a phrase using the grammar and the lexicon. The recognizer accepts the string or rejects it, depending upon the criteria established for denoting well-formed strings. The analyzer associates the input string with its structure, according to the grammar. The transducer associates the string with alternate structures that reflect the domain of discourse. The components are summarized in two sections: syntactic parsing and semantic processing.

Without going into theoretical analysis of the subject matter, it is possible to describe the two most productive methods of syntactic parsing: Augmented Transition Networks (ATNs) and Chart Parsing.

There is a significant amount of expectation inherent in natural language. When a person hears or reads the article "the," for example, an adjective or noun is expected next in line. An ATN is a network of nodes (called states) that reflect the situation. One node denotes the start and one or more nodes serve as a finish. When a word of a given category is encountered, the word is consumed and the system goes into a new state. Overall, an ATN reflects a sentence and sub networks reflect constituents of a sentence, such as noun phrases, verb phrases, and so forth. The process is top-down and internal registers are used to store contextual information and direct the flow. Highly complex grammars can be parsed with ATNs.

Chart parsing is a bottom-up alternative to the use of ATNs; both are based theoretically on a linguistic concept known as Phrase Structure Grammars (PSGs). With chart processing, the text is recognized and assembled word-by-word. Words are combined into syntactic entities, eventually resulting in complete sentences. Varying combinations of words are constructed with the ultimate objective of synthesizing a feasible interpretation. Chart processing can provide a partial analysis even if a complete grammatical sentence in not available.

Phrases are constructed with chart processing that span increasingly larger sections of a sentence. Accordingly, it may generate alternate interpretations of a sentence without providing any means of deciding the preferred result.

Semantic Processing

The best-known methods of assessing the semantic properties of a sentence are case grammars and contextual analysis. The objective is obvious: to control the level of ambiguity in natural language.

A case grammar can be viewed as either a detailed syntax of a generalized semantics based on the verb of a phrase or sentence. The value of case grammars is that for most verbs, a frame can be defined. The slots of the frame reflect the subject of the verb, object, and so forth. Case grammars are sometimes known as "case frames."

Conceptual analysis (CA) takes the notion of case grammar one step further by defining 11 distinct primitive actions, normally in discourse. Two common examples of CA primitives are ATRANS and PTRANS. ATRANS represents an abstract relation, such as the transfer of ownership, and PTRANS is used to denote the physical transfer of an object. Thus two equivalent sentences, such as:

John sold Mary a book
Mary bought a book from John

Would be represented is the same way using conceptual analysis using the primitive ATRANS. Similarly, the sentence "John went home" would be described with PTRANS.

In conceptual analysis, each primitive has "expectations" that are expected, so in fact, they can play a key role in a larger unit of description called a script. Most everyday actions, such as going to a restaurant or the post office can be modeled with an appropriate script.

There is a high level of activity in the DP world and in AI circles on the topic of natural language processing. The reasons are clear. Natural language is understood by practically everybody, and it is self-updating. The bandwidth of natural language is high, and it presents a low initial barrier to end users of DP systems. Natural language systems lend to human adaption as writers and end users quickly learn the sentences that succeed, in a figurative sense.

Vision

Recent programs in locomotion and robotics have created a new need for a close look at vision systems. After years of only marginal success, AI researchers have agreed that the problem is much more difficult than they originally thought. Existing industrial vision systems look at high contrast scenes and compare the resulting lines and dots to existed images. These systems use a hierarchy of representations that allow processing of visual information in many intermediate stages to traverse the conceptual distance between input signals and cognitive symbols.

After a quarter of a century or more of development, vision research has become a major subfield of AI. Early systems were concerned with image recognition in the forms of edge elements and primitive data objects, and image manipulation such as scaling and rotation. A cognitive approach subsequently surfaced that emphasized symbolic processing and knowledge representation. The later direction led to notion of abstraction and a vision hierarchy.

AI components in vision systems utilize texture and motion to key into semantic data structures that promote a "context of vision," analogous to the methods of conceptual analysis. The research is close to psychology, as was the case with natural language processing and a "model driven" approach that is currently fashionable.

Using the human brain as a model, scientists outside of the mainstream of traditional AI have built vision systems that combine technologies from electronics, robotics, and computer science. The key to success would appear to be the development of special hardware units for vision.

Connectionism

One of the most severe limitations of natural language and vision systems is computation speed. Von Neumann machines are too slow for sophisticated practical work, and most AI researchers agree that parallelism is the answer. There are several well-known ways of achieving parallelism; the emphasis here is on a rebirth of area of AI known as connectionism. Parallelism is surveyed briefly as a related technology.

The Human Brain

The human brain has traditionally been regarded as a sophisticated switching network consisting of billions of processing elements, known as neurons that communicate through electrical impulses. Since the 1970s, however, neuroscientists have determined that neurons work together in large groups and interact through electromagnetic fields. This sheds a new light on cooperative behavior, since the synchronous behavior of thousands of neurons that are continually and instantaneously reflected back to affect subsequent activity. This is clearly a new direction in associative behavior and has led computer designers to pursue a new type of computer – the Connection Machine. Even though, the notion of a connection machine has not been

totally accepted by the business and computer communities, the concept is certainly worthy of note.

There is some history and value to this direction of research. Scientists at Carnegie-Mellon University have developed a software simulation of a novel computer architecture known as the Boltzmann Machine. Each processor is connected to hundreds of other and is either "on" or "off" at any moment. The links between a processor and its neighbors area assigned numerical "weights" that can be either positive or negative. To decide whether to change its state, each processor sums the weights of the inputs it receives from other currently active processors and compares this sum with a threshold value. It then calculates its own state accordingly to a probabilistic decision rule. If the sum is above the threshold value, the processor the processor turns on half of the time. Because the activity of the individual processors is probabilistic, the behavior of the network as a whole can be analyzed with the same statistical formulas that describe the kinetic behavior of gases. For this reason, the simulated machine was named after Ludwig Boltzmann (1844-1906), as Austrian physicist whose research on gas thermodynamics led to the field of statistical mechanics. Information in the Boltzmann Machine is stored not in the individual processors but in their connections, which are represented mathematically by the numerical weights. Machines of this gender are relatively easy to conceptualize and serve was term projects for students. Programs are relatively short to write and give the students a keen sense of accomplishment in

the field of artificial intelligence. Petri Nets are a commonly used production vehicle for this type of project.

The Connection Machine

The basic computing speed of the brain is a few milliseconds, so that a reasonably complex task, such as recognizing a face, which takes about half of a second, is computed in roughly 100 steps. The number of sequential time steps to perform the same task in an abstract AI system runs into the millions. Clearly, the brain is a highly parallel device. Moreover, large symbolic structures cannot be passed through the neural structure in binary form with the 100-step restriction. Based on analyses, such as these, a "connection" model of the brain is hypothesized that employs connections among the units that go far beyond the neural structure of the brain in its traditional form.

Parallelism can be designed into a computer system at various levels. Low-level parallelism is achieved by pipelining techniques, interleaved storage, and parallel functional units. All of these techniques hare transparent to conventional in conventional software. A higher level of parallelism, on the other hand, normally involves the interaction of several closely coupled processors connected in the form of an array or a network. Thus, the multiple processors can cooperate on a computational task but operate in tandem.

Two methodologies stand out in the above discussion: dataflow computers and connection machines. A salient

characteristic of traditional and parallel computers, as discussed thus far, is that they are process driven. What this means is that procedures, - i.e., machine code, normally written as statements in some programming language – essentially run the show. Moreover, processes request data when they need it and blindly go about doing what they do. The problem is obvious. Data is not always readily available when needed, and this causes computational delays and thwarts effective parallelism.

In a dataflow computer, the flow of data is optimized. Each processor receives data packets from other processors. When a process has the data it needs, it performs a calculation and sends the results on to another processor. Thus, each processor is supplied with a storage area with instructions on what do with the data and associated interconnection ports. Data flow programs are written as a "map" describing the flow of computation. Software is used to convert a high level description into instructions for the constituent processors.

The Connection Machine no longer exists but is a useful computer but its design supplements the story of artificial intelligence. It is a non-von Neumann computer, often called non-Von, wherein each processor is connected to the remainder through a 4,096 switching station and 24,576 trunk lines. The Connection Machine has scanned three months of Reuters News – 16,00 articles in all-in 1/20 of a second. The operational speed of the computer is in excess of one billion instructions per second equivalent to a Cray supercomputer at a fraction the cost.

Technology

In spite of a considerable amount of discussion, the notion of intelligence appears to be one of those things that is difficult to define bit is readily recognizable in practice. When does an object possess intelligence? Clearly, there are fast minds, to use the term loosely, and slow minds. Moreover, there is more than one type of mind. There are differences between adults, between children, and between and adults and children. There are differences between humans, dogs, monkeys, and other animals. There are cross-cultural differences, and there are differences between intelligent machines. There doesn't seem to be a clear boundary betwee what is intelligent and what is not. It is possible, on the other hand, that the field of Computer Science has provided us with a unique approach to the quest for intelligence. The concept of a virtual machine, defined as an abstract structure that can support diverse computational states and processes, is a useful paradigm for identifying the boundaries of artificial intelligence.

Dimensions of Intelligence

A virtual machine can reside in a physical machine without having to be that machine. Similarly, the same virtual machine can be installed on two different physical machines, and two different virtual machines can reside in the same physical

machine. It follows that different virtual machines can have different properties.

In the realm of AI, one virtual machine can play chess, another can support oil prospecting, another can perform as a medical assistant, and yet another function as a financial advisor. Then if we look at the space of all such virtual machines, we get a realistic picture of what it is that artificial intelligence is supposed to be. There is no clear boundary between possessing intelligence and not possessing intelligence. The dimensions of intelligence do not form a smooth continuum but are marked with many discontinuities. Some AI virtual machines could appear to exhibit a reasonable level of intelligence, such as an expert system, while others, such a pick-and-pace robots, hardly seem deserving of the term "intelligent."

Without making a claim to absolute completeness, it appears as though the following AI technologies could adequately represent the dimensions of intelligence in a hypothetical AI virtual machine: Knowledge representation (KR), reasoning (R), vision (V), pattern recognition (PD), natural language processing (NLP), and speech processing (SP).

As the dimensions multiply, an AI system gives the appearance of being more intelligent, and a quick estimate is that the effect is exponential. The field of artificial intelligence is commonly viewed in terms of its applications and not in its technologies. It is common to read of AI applications with interesting names, such as MYCIN, HACKER, and ACTOR. The list is old but the point

has been made. This is unfortunate since the technology of AI is a knowledge domain.

In reality, the computational facilities often used in AI work is means of solving a problem and not a complete set of AI applications. Thus, the domain of AI tools spans the set of applications. The two most significant technologies are knowledge representation and reasoning.

Knowledge Representation

There is a concept in AI known as the primacy of knowledge. What this implies is that the ability of a system to perform a task is a function of the knowledge that the system has about the task – regardless of how cleverly the system reasons about it. In this regard, AI is an empirical art and not a theory. It is the engineering procedure of building tools, evaluating them, tearing them down, and repeating the process. Currently, there are elements of a theory in AI and eventually it will have a theory as in Biology. An emphasis on knowledge representation (KR) makes sense, because most of the world's work is thinking, which is composed of problem solving, concept formulation, and knowledge processing.

In its traditional form, knowledge is more static than data. Two varieties of knowledge are commonly recognized: factual knowledge, which is acquired through learning, and heuristic knowledge, which is gained through experience. It is not a joke that heuristic knowledge is known as "The Art of Good Guessing."

It follows that capturing the art of good guessing is commonly regarded as knowledge engineering.

Human knowledge is commonly regarded as passive information recorded in books and periodicals and facts stored in the minds of individuals. Through their existence, many structures created by society ar implicit in the design of those structures. In the field of computer technology, computer programs use algorithms that operate on stored data. An expert system, commonly known as a knowledge system, is a program that operates on a class of stored data. Collectively, an expert system is comprised of the information and a set of algorithms.

When an expert system is created, the main task is the modeling of the expert. People have only limited capability to construct long chains of deductions and have only limited knowledge, at any one point in time. This is a form of limited human rationality.

Because of limited human rationality, representation is a key issue, because it spans the various steps of the inference process. One categorization of knowledge representation is that it is a stylized version of the world. It is stylized because the method(s) employed depend of the objects to be represented and the expected processing that will be performed on the objects that are represented.

Engineering Approach

In the human brain, knowledge is stored as neurochemical structures, electromagnetic fields, electrical impulses, and probably other unknown methods. Ii will take scientists many years to sort out precisely how the brain stores information and, in fact, how it uses that information. As a practical endeavor, an attempt to model the brain is simply not effective. AI researchers have alternately selected to "engineer" a few methods that work for the kinds of problems encountered in today's world. As a practical example, airplanes do not fly like birds. Engineering is necessary.

The engineering approach to knowledge representation would first involve a look at the problem domain. In the case of artificial intelligence, the basic needs include taxonomies, inheritance, constraints, and uncertainty.

Taxonomy refers to classification, as in the following example:

> Cows are mammals.
> Mammals are vertebrates.
> Mammals suckle their young.
> Vertebrates have backbones.

Taxonomy, in its most general sense, is the concept through which knowledge is stored.

Inheritance, albeit related to taxonomy, involves the capability of obtaining attribute values through a hierarchical structure

without explicitly stating them, as in the following case from propositional logic:

All birds have feathers.
Tweety is a bird.
Therefore, Tweety has feathers.

In this case, an object inherited an attribute value from a more general class. Inheritance provides more than just a means of picking up attribute values from a superclass. It encourages and facilitates effective organization of knowledge – something the brain does automatically in its magical ways.

The notion of constraint refers to the process by which a value is known if its associated values are known. In the case of Ohm's Law of the form:

$$V=IR$$

for electrical resistors, a third value can readily be computed if the other two values are known. In advanced knowledge systems, a constraint value is encoded in the slot of a frame and is available through a method attached to that slot.

The concept of uncertainty is fundamental to all knowledge. Heretofore in AI and expert systems, a tacit assumption has been made that all knowledge statements are true. For special cases, such as medical diagnosis, certainty factors or belief functions were simply 'tacked on.' A modern look at knowledge

representation should be based on the uncertainty that is inherent in most knowledge systems.

Production Systems

The most widely and extensively tested means of representing an expert system is to use the concept of a production system developed in the U.S.A. in he 1970s and applied in one form or another in most large-scale expert systems. A production system is used for the representation of knowledge and for AI reasoning.

A production system is a set of condition-action pairs, called production rules that are used to represent an inference procedure. Accordingly, the form of a production rule is:

IF <condition> THEN <action>

The "conditions" are ascertained from input values that are facts in the knowledge base and from previous "actions."

Associated with an inference procedure is a short-term memory, termed the context, the long-term memory called the knowledge base, and a set of rules and a rule interpreter, sometimes known as the inference engine. In French AI, the inference engine is called the motor, with the obvious analogy to the functioning of an automobile. The motor drives an automobile in the same manner that an inference engine drives an expert system.

The inference engine, which is actually a software module, has access to the rule base, the context, and the knowledge base.

The engine operates by finding all rules for which the condition part is true. A control strategy is applied to select the rule to be found, and the process is again repeated. The "action" can take the form of an end-user interaction, the execution of a hardware or software function, or the computation of a value that is added to the context.

A production system can be used to store knowledge in a way that is functionally analogous to tables, structures, hierarchies, nets, frames, and so forth. Each element of knowledge is represented is represented by a rule. A typical production rule of this type might be:

IF age = 30 THEN risk level is 5

Clearly, this information could have been stored equally well in a table. It is a matter of record that in expert systems with thousands of production rules, many of the rules are used only to store knowledge.

The basic methods of knowledge representation are natural language, predicate logic, frames, semantic nets, methods, and blackboards. Most methods are use in combination. Conceptual dependency graphs are considered to be a special case; they have been introduced previously.

Natural Language, Relations, and Predicate Logic

A natural language representation of knowledge would take the form of a normal sentence, such as

John gave Mary the book

This knowledge could be represented in an unambiguous manner is the form of a relation, such as

GIVE (JOHN, MARY, BOOK)

Similarly, the following items represent the same ideas:

John is a programmer
OCCUPATION (JOHN, PROGRAMMER)

Mary is a lawyer
OCCUPATION (MARY, LAWYER)

and

John's address is 37 Maple Street
ADDRESS (JOHN, 37-MAPLE)

Items in parenthesis are attribute values. Items, such as GIVE, OCCUPATION, and ADDRESS are relations, as in database theory. In predicate logic relations are known as "predicates." Expert systems and logic programming languages can use predicates in the reasoning process.

A semantic net is a relational model among objects, classes, and attributes, as suggested by the following diagram:

Tweety IS-A Canary IS-A Bird HAS-PART Wings

In this case, "IS-A" and "HAS-PART" are relations, and the other entities are an object (Tweety), classes (Canary and Bird), and an attribute (Wings). Clearly, objects may have attributes, attributes can have attributes, and so forth.

Semantic nets are particularly useful for expert systems, because entities in a net can be described by frames and can inherit attribute values from other entities in the net. Moreover, objects may participate in several relations, providing complete generality as a representative scheme.

Method

A method is a computational procedure attached to a slot, which is a data structure in AI. A reference to a slot causes the associated procedure to be invoked, which computes the needed value. The notion of a method is a necessary concept in AI. It appears that only two facilities are necessary to allow and expert system to work: a frame and at least one method. A knowledge base is stored in a frame with hierarchies, so that inference can be performed by the methods.

Blackboard

A blackboard is a knowledge structure that facilitates the concurrent, and perhaps cooperative, activity of multiple reasoning agents. The current state of a problem is represented in its blackboard. Each reasoning agent possesses a specialty and applies his or her area of expertise to an appropriate part of the problem as a solution unfolds on the blackboard.

Reasoning

Reasoning is commonly understood to be the process of inferring one fact from another. In reality, inference can come in three forms: deduction, abduction, and induction. Inference methods are inherent in forward and backward chaining.

Inference

The basis of production systems and much of the current crop of expert systems is the process of deduction. Deduction takes the form:

IF a THEN b

a is true

Infer that b is true

This is a rule in logic called Modus Ponens, which produces "legal inference." Abduction takes the form:

> IF a THEN b
> b is true
> _____
> Infer that a is true

This is a rule in logic called Modus Tollens. Abduction does not product "legal inference," and is a means of generating a questionable explanation of observation. Abduction can lead to the wrong conclusion but is very useful and often necessary. Abduction is often pertinent to medical diagnosis. The final form of inference is induction. Induction is essentially the search for patterns in observed data and takes the form:

> P a is true
> P b is true
> ...
> _____
> Infer for all x, P x is true

Induction reflects the process of learning, which is in its infancy in AI.

Forward Chaining

One method of using a production or rule-based system is to reason from first principles or premises, as they are normally

known. This process, known as forward chaining, starts with a fact and then finds a rule whose premise is satisfied by the fact.

One means of conceptualizing forward chaining is that it is a means of responding to new facts and simulating actions. Accordingly, forward chaining operates somewhat a s follows:

- The interpreter looks at the first of the new facts.
- All of the rules are identified to which that fact is a premise.
- A check is made whether all the premises for the flagged rules are verified.
- For all verified rules, the specified actions are taken, often by updating the context.
- The process is repeated with the next item from the set of facts.

The interpreter in question is the "production rule interpreter," which is commonly a part of an expert system environment.

The notion of a control strategy frequently arises because the order in which the interpreter runs through the production rules can determine the results that are obtained. Some of the strategies commonly mentioned are to apply the last rule used, the highest priority rule, and the rule that refers to the value most recently added to the context.

Forward chaining is particularly useful for AI problems that ivovel diagnosis systems and "what to do" applications.

Backward Chaining

In contradistinction to forward chaining, backward chaining starts with a conclusion to be established and works toward the premises or conditions that would cause it to happen. Backward chaining is tantamount to breaking a problem down into sub-goals, the sub-goals into lower sub-goals, and so forth.

Backward chaining is particularly useful for AI applications in which a goal of some kind is to be reached and a good strategy is needed to get there. During backward chaining, a hypothesis is established, perhaps it is even selected by the AI system itself. The interpreter scans its rule base to see if its conditions are correctly established as facts. If so, then the hypothesis is proved. If the conditions of that rule occur as conclusions (i.e., actions) of another rule, then the conditions for that rule are similarly inspected. Thus, the system works backwards until the truth or falsity of all relevant conditions have been ascertained.

The process of backward chaining is summarize as follows:

- A hypothesis to be satisfied is selected.
- A rule for this hypothesis is found.
- A check is made to see if the conditions for this rule are true.
- It any of the conditions is a conclusion to some other rule, then backward chaining, as described in this list, is applied to each of those rules and the process is repeated until the set of initial conditions are reached.

Forward and backward chaining can utilize the same knowledge base, since the inference process is independent of the production rule structure.

Explanation Capability

It is normally the case that an expert system is designed to interact with an end user. Certainly, exceptions exist as with expert systems that are designed and developed to control things, such as computer systems and airplanes.

An expert system can interact with the end user in one or more of the following instances:

- For entering facts into the contextual memory
- For stating hypotheses, as in backward chaining
- In response to a query to the user
- To invoke the explanation capability

Items one through three are straightforward and could normally be expected in an information system of any kind. The explanation capability Is unique.

The explanation capability permits an expert system to run through the chain of reasoning used in an inference process and effectively explain its actions. This is particularly useful for training environments and in critical systems – such as medical diagnosis.

Many expert systems are justified solely on the basis of the explanation facility. The underlying thinking is that if an expect system turns out to be unusable by domain experts, it can always be used for training purposes.

Applications

It is usefully to summarize developments in AI technology prior to covering AI applications. The major areas of developments are:

- New data structures for representing things about the world
- New algorithms to represent facts
- Advanced programming environments
- New computer architectures
- Project management
- Enhanced methods for human/computer interaction
- Special applications of AI technology

The developments do not guarantee success, but the lack of them may be associated with failure. The areas of development are: reliable service, user interface, complete toolbox, and the application must demonstrate intelligence.

AI Technologies

The AI technologies mentioned previously include:

- Robotics,
- Vision
- Pattern recognition

- Speech
- Natural languages
- Complexity interface

The various technologies are used primarily in natural language technologies, and expert systems.

Natural Language

There is not much in the area of natural language that is relevant to the current discussion of artificial intelligence. Robotics and speech are superfluous at this time. Vision and pattern recognition are questionable. The technology exists for well-defined jobs, such as visual processing of securities, but is available only as standalone systems.

In modern AI, natural language is well represented.

Natural language is almost as problematical, but there are three general applications that are relevant:

- A natural language interface to a database system
- Analysis of a document composed in natural language for subsequent analysis or rerouting
- A machine translation package as part of a comprehensive management information system

Question-and-answer systems and natural language interfaces to expert systems have been created in the laboratory but are not viable products at this time.

The overall lack of success by the AI community with natural language processing brings up an important question: Is natural language really natural for the computer? For DP applications, as we currently know them, the answer is clearly 'no.' Moreover, natural language has a narrow bandwidth and should be supplanted by high bandwidth systems based on high resolution graphs and enhanced visual systems.

Expert Systems

The subject of expert systems is commonly regarded as a branch of artificial intelligence based on software technology, even though specially constructed hardware may be used in the process. An expert system is essentially a computer program; in fact, the dependence on programming is so great that artificial intelligence is sometimes viewed as a new way of doing programming.

An expert system uses explicitly represented knowledge and computational inference procedures to solve problems that normally require human knowledge and judgment. The subject matter to which an expert system is applied is referred to as its domain. Thus, knowledge relevant to a given task is known as domain knowledge and the associated human specialist is called a domain expert

In conventional computer programs, the knowledge and control are intermixed. In an expert system, the knowledge is in the form of facts, and rules are distinct from the mechanism that uses the knowledge to draw inferences. Thus, the behavior of an expert system can be changed through modifications of the facts or the rules.

Expert systems are based on a symbolic representation of real-world objects and symbolic inferences and are particularity useful in three cases. First, human expertise is not always available. Second, expertise can be applied more uniformly and more rapidly than with a network of experts. Lastly, an expert system provides a common knowledge base that can evolve dynamically as the system is used for not only one but many applications.

It is customary to leverage the cost of an expert system against the cost of a human export, and in many cases, the concept of an expert assistant can be employed to more profitably utilize the skills of the human. Another key point is that an expert system can normally explain its behavior and can accordingly be used for justification and training.

Expert Systems Architecture

As covered previously, the application software for an export system must contain a knowledge base, and inference engine, and an end-user interface. In fact, any worthwhile software must contain the three elements. The names of the pieces may be different, but the idea must be the same. This is the most important element in this book. In AI, the generic software entities are normally implemented through the following hardware and software products:

- An AI shell
- An AI language
- An AI environment

The AI shell incorporates the inference engine and implicitly specifies the method of knowledge representation. The AI language is the vehicle through which the AI shell and knowledge base are implemented. The AI environment provides the method of display, bit-mapped graphics, and the editor. One typical AI shell with a historical perspective is KEE for knowledge engineering environment. Its AI language is LISP, and the typical environment is the Lambda LISP Machine.

AI Programming Languages

The two most well known AI programming languages are LISP and Prolog. LISP refers to list processing, and Prolog refers to programming in logic. Both languages are exceedingly powerful and are reasonably easy to learn. Python is commonly used in modern AI.

Topics

Exactly what constitutes AI is still an open item. Two types of AI have been identified: Weak AI and Strong AI. Weak AI focuses on specific problems, such as specific games, giving directions, and specific medical diagnosis. Strong AI focuses on how humans solve problems and how to apply that knowledge in a computer environment. With weak AI, a set of programs is told how to do a specific task. With strong AI, the computer determines what it has to do to be learning. Weak AI exists today. Strong AI is under development. As covered in the first section of this book, strong AI involves the development of algorithms that can solve a class of problems usually involving a collection of data sets. Expert systems are a typical example of strong AI. If the development of algorithms involves expert systems in its most general sense, the methods involve modeling of how the brain functions and is known as deep learning, usually implements as neural networks. With neural networks, the software takes input and generates output with an algorithm that runs through a series of networks – such like the human brain functions.

Neural Networks

A typical neural network is a connected set od nodes organized somewhat like the human brain. They are used to recognize

relationship s between relatively large sets of data. Typical applications of neural networks include: medical diagnosis, controlling robots, visual recognition, face recognition, running complex mechanical equipment, controlling complex agriculture, banking and portfolio management, learning and playing board games, racist history, military strategy, dieting and weight control, cleaning, painting, and just about every activity usually performed by human beings.

Robots and Original Standalone AI Applications

The Google Corporation has invested in an extensive program in Artificial Intelligence that employs technology in all areas of the discipline. There is no limit to Google's achievement, that includes neural networks, robot technology, control facilities, art and design methods, and modern biological systems. Here are some of the examples: training and learning, learn how to detect and play electronic games, creating and understanding stories, prediction of human behavior, racist behavior, spacecraft and military behavior, early warning and control systems, cancer detection, medical drug design, Improved MRI scans, genetics and autism, interspace behavior and control, and warming and agriculture. There are, of course, additional areas of investigation.

Technological Singularity

Some artificial intelligence researchers have expressed the idea that as AI systems expanded in scope and flexibility, they would eventually take over the human civilization. AI systems

are currently designed and built created by humans, but as the systems become smarter, they would be able to design future AI systems that would be able to build systems that would surpass human intelligence. Then, those "smart" systems could run away with civilization. They would be beyond the control of their human creators.

Many AI people think that a runaway set of intelligent systems taking over their own design would be totally ridiculous. Large software systems contain millions of lines of code and never get bug-free versions in their lifetimes. Some software design and builders, such as IBM, have exotically developed systems that produce nearly bug free code, but still need the end users to help in the checkout process. Some software develop systems with bugs in them and rely primarily on the end users to find errors.

The point when artificial intelligence systems take over the world is known as the singularity or more precisely the technological singularity. Some authors have even written books on the subject. However, the subject is just an idea, since no one has shown how to create the singularity. Polls of computer scientists have been made to determine just how feasible that idea is. Some well-known that at the singularity would result in human extinction. Four polls in the 2012 and 2013 time period were made and there was a one in two chance that we would have a singularity by 2050.

To start out, one would need a pretty large computer to achieve a singularity and that would be quite an achievement in a society

where computers can barely recognize a cow. It's a humorous endeavor to think about a singularity and apply Moore's Law, which states that computer power doubles every ten years. This may not be completely accurate since the source is Wiki. (https://en_m.wikipedia.org/wiki/Technological_singularity.) Actually, the entire article is based on this Wiki report.

Several philosophers, computer people, and writers have state that there is no reason to believe in a artificial intelligence singularity, and they essentially doubt that will happen. (See the Wiki for comments by such academics.)

Machine Intelligence and Learning

Machine intelligence and learning reflects a computer system that exhibits behavior that would be classified as intelligent if performed by a human agent. That computer system would be known as an intelligent agent, and that field of study is termed artificial intelligence. Some researchers refer to AI, as it is usually called, as that which hasn't been done yet, even though that term doesn't seem to make sense in today's computer world. That would imply that an intelligent agent should, in fact, perform a certain amount of learning.

Some researchers feel as though AI can be achieved when human intelligence can be described in sufficient detail that a machine can be made to simulate it. One of the early artificial intelligent applications is "compute chess" wherein the program emulates a human chess player. Some AI applications can learn

how to play a game and win by learning how to operate without human intervention.

In general, AI researchers feel that any problem that can be solved by a human can be developed as an AI application, and the challenger is to have the AI program learn by itself how to play. That is why machine learning is one of the most important concepts in artificial intelligence.

Other disciplines can be related to machine intelligence, such as advanced statistical techniques, which is termed deep learning. There are several topics related to machine intelligence and learning:

- Reasoning and problem solving
- Knowledge representation
- Knowledge engineering
- Qualification
- Natural language
- Creativity
- General intelligence

The various subjects are held together through a Web Ontology Language that can be used to represent what exists.

AI is relevant to any task that can demonstrate intelligence. As before, when a term (or technique) reaches mainstream, it is no longer considered artificial intelligence. This is the AI effect.

Here are some worthy applications: Healthcare, Automotive, Finance, and Video Games. There are three basic questions:

- Is artificial general intelligence possible? Can a machine solve any problem that a human can solve?
- Are intelligent machines dangerous?
- Can a machine be intelligent? Can it "think?"

The questions are answered in https://en.m.wikipedia.org/wiki/Artificial_intelligence

The Advisor Paradigm

An expert system is characterized by a database of facts and a logical engine for exploiting the facts in a purposeful manner. The logical engine takes good advantage of the available information so that the output of the system is considerably more than what would ordinarily be implied strictly by the input. The data and the inference programs give the system an air of being an expert.

One of the most illustrative examples of an expert system is the well-known wine advisor. The user enters a brief description of an entrée, such as chicken with cream sauce, and the system yields a small wine selection, such as Chardonnay or Montrachet – depending of course upon the current contents of the wine cellar. Naturally, there is more to the story. The entrée has certain characteristics that are determined by a database search. The

characteristics are then used by an inference mechanism during a "run" of the system to generate the attributes of a suitable wine, such as color, taste, and strength (i.e., light, heavy, etc.) In a second database operation, the wine attributes are mapped into a "variety" of wine. Finally, a selection is made from the database that represents the contents of the wine cellar.

Similar advisors have been constructed in the financial community and in the nuclear industry – to name only a few. In an investment advisor, for example, an investor's profile is mapped into a well-defined, but much larger, set of investment characteristics using a database operation. Again, an inference mechanism is used; in this case, it generates a portfolio structure that serves as input to a database search operation yielding a set of investment options. A typical portfolio structure might be: 60% equities, 35% bonds, and 5% gold. The output set would be a small selection of instruments in selected currencies.

In the nuclear industry, a collection of physical events occurring in an emergency situation would be translated by an expert system into a set of instructions to an operator. As before, the processing sequence includes an initial database search operation, an inference procedure, and then a final database selection to generate the needed instructions. The examples typify the "advisor paradigm."

The advisor paradigm is characterized by the following set of actions occurring in essentially the order given:

- A relatively small set of input values are entered into the system via and end user interaction or as the result of a physical event.
- The input values are expanded into the particulars for a certain problem domain via a database search process.
- The particulars are mapped into a set of descriptors via an inference mechanism that can take the form of a set of if-then rules and a logical engine, a neural network, a pattern matching operation, a mathematical function, or possibly logic program.\
- The descriptors are used as key values in a subsequent database search operation to yield the results for that problem.

Clearly, the salient properties of the advisor paradigm are the initial database operation, the inference (or mapping) process, and the final database search. The two database operations are obviously to different structures. Each of these components can be replicated, as required by a particular problem and its problem solver, but the general structure of the paradigm is evident without necessarily going into ore detail. In fact, most expert systems operate in precisely this manner, even though the emphasis has conventionally been on the rules and knowledge-based parts of the model.

The advisor paradigm is independent of the mode of representation; this fact is tacitly understood and is inherent in the notion of a paradigm. Representation is dependent upon a specific instantiation of the model. If the cells in a spreadsheet application are the source of information, then the retrieval and inference operations are related to that framework. If the inference processes are implemented as LISP or Prolog programs, then the particulars and descriptors are constrained by the corresponding ad hoc data structures. To sum up, the method of representation is determined by the underlying problem domain and computational framework. This explains to a limited degree why a lot more "advisors" are not floating around in the industrial, academic, and governmental communities. The ultimate objective is clear: to make the benefits of the advisor paradigm available in a general-purpose format.

Another consideration that complicates the picture is the existence of uncertainty in most areas dealings with human affairs. Uncertainty has been the Achilles heel of the artificial intelligence community, since a practical system for problem solving should take the uncertainty of information or the uncertainty of the reasoning process into consideration. Naturally, we would like to have the mechanisms in place for dealing effectively with both forms of uncertainty, even though all of the features may not be needed for a particular problem situation. It is indeed one thing to map an entrée of beef into a wine descriptor in a deterministic sense, such as:

beef -> strong red meat -> dry heavy red wine -> ...

and quite another to introduce the notion of uncertainty, as in:

small lump -> (((healthy, tests))),0.6),((healthy, tests, sick),0.4))

->... -> ((home, office).0.56)

The notation in the latter example is intended to demonstrate that a small lump is mapped into the conditions of healthy or tests with a certainty of 0.6 and into the conditions of healthy or tests or sick with a certainty factor of 0.4. Total comprehension here is not expected, but is given to indicate that uncertainty is complicated. The stage is obviously set. A system for managing uncertainty

In the wine and medical examples, there is relatively little risk in the advisory process, and gives us the opportunity of focusing on the initial database operation. The process represents a translation between the external work=ld of the end user to the internal world of the automated problem solver In the wine advisor, for example, the indicator of beef is mapped into a set of attributes with which the expert system can work, as in:

beef -> strong red meat

or in its generic form:

indicator -> meaning

The notion of an indicator is well-established in organized society in the form of symbols, variables, synonyms, and abbreviations. It is commonplace to have an indicator, such as successful, that is associated with a substantial set of characteristics, such as aggressive, confident, intelligent, and focused. Indicators can have different meanings to different people' however, which preserves the role of the expert. In the absence of uncertainly, and indicator has a definite meaning. In the presence of uncertainty, an indicator might mean something, and the degree to which an expert believes the assertion is known as its certainty value, or as its the certainty factor, as it is sometimes called. Thus, the indicator in the presence of uncertainty is a clue to the validity of an assertion; it becomes evidence when combined with its meaning and a certainty value, or in its generic form:

Evidence: indicator -> meaning with certainly value.

An obvious consideration applies to the notion of evidence. As in common everyday usage, a fact "is entered as evidence" only when it is relevant to the case under consideration. An analogous caveat applies to the methods contained here, and a means is presented for constraining the relevancy of information.

PART II

Service Elements

CHAPTER 7

Special Introduction

———————— ∿ ————————

A service is generally regarded as work performed by one person or group that benefits another, and the concepts are systematically applied to products, as well. But what, exactly, is service. It is generally regarded as a provider/client interaction in which both parties participate and both parties obtain some benefit from the relationship. A service is a form of activity, consumed at the point of production in which the provider and client exchange information and adopt differing roles in the process. Service is a prevalent activity that is applicable in principle to business, education, government, and diverse personal endeavors. Many organizations have been drastically transformed through the use of services, because it is often the case that an outside service provider can perform an activity more efficiently and more effectively than can be performed locally. This is known as outsourcing and the work can be exceedingly complex or routinely simple. The concepts are general in nature and apply equally well to medical treatment and automobile repair, to name a couple of examples.

To set the stage for further discussion, the study of Service relates to traditional services (such as medical provisioning, banking, insurance, and a variety of personal services), Internet and informational services, business organization and operations,

consulting, government, education, software development, and even sports and recreation – to name only a few areas. One person has described the operation of the human body as a collection of services and another has developed a DNA of services.

Service is an interesting subject in its own right. The New York Times author and writer Thomas Friedman set the stage for the subject matter as it relates to globalization in the winter of 2006 in his book entitled *The World is Flat*. Clearly, globalization is a key area of engagement, with regard to Service, and there appears to be a large amount of international interest in the subject matter.

We are additionally listing several interesting components of the subject of Service, to promote further discussion:

> Service concepts
> Service systems
> Information services
> Service management
> Service technology
> Service architecture
> Service business

There is a high level of interest in Service since it has the potential to change the way we think about and subsequently view the new world order. Many persons feel that the subject of Service will eventually change the predominant economic focus from products to services?

Responding to this situation, the IBM Corporation initiated a project in the years 2005-2006 to develop a science of services. The project has resulted in tidal wave of activity within businesses and universities to study the subject and develop academic programs. The generic title for programs of this type is Service Science, Management, and Engineering (SSME) with Service Science as its basis. Corresponding academic programs are already in place in many universities in the US, England, and Germany.

Since service is the cornerstone of most modern businesses, there is a high level of interest in the subject by persons from business, government, and education. The subject of service science has been addressed in papers in most business and computer conferences, usually in the area of service management and service marketing because a clear description of exactly what constitutes Service has not heretofore been available.

CHAPTER 8

Understanding Services

The subject of services is in the news, because it is the up and coming discipline for the 22nd century. It is more significant than technology, entrepreneurship, business growth, and innovation. In fact, services encompass all of the subjects mentioned. Services are important to people in business, government, education, health care and management, religion, military, scientific research, engineering, and other endeavors that are too numerous to mention. The subject is of interest to providers and consumers of services, alike. In fact, most service providers – be they individuals, businesses, governments, and so forth – are also consumers of services.

Employment And The Service Sector

Today, most of us are employed in services. Typical examples are doctors, dentists, lawyers, teachers, entertainers, news people, dry cleaners, and maintenance workers. Actually, this should not be a surprise, since much of what we do in everyday life involves using services.

Service activity is characterized by the fact that the results are usually intangible, meaning in this case that an artifact of some

sort is not produced as a result of a service experience, as it is in the manufacture of products.

SERVICE – A PERSONAL DIMENSION

Most of us want to do better – in our jobs, education, business, professions, and so forth, and when we purchase services, it is really important that we get the best service for our time and money. But without a clear understanding of exactly what it is that constitutes a service, what differentiates one service from another, and how services operate and interoperate, continuous improvement will be a never-ending process of trial and error.

The concept of service has its roots in economic activities that are classified as extractive, secondary, and services. *Extractive* refers to agriculture, mining, forestry, fishing, and so forth. *Secondary* refers to manufacturing and processing. *Services* refer to everything else, usually subdivided into domestic, trade and commerce, information services, and personal. This is a very general definition intended for the reporting by the government of economic conditions. In order to get a handle on services, we need better definitions.

A *service* is a provider/client interaction that creates and captures value. A unique characteristic of services, unlike agriculture and manufacturing, is that both parties participate in the transaction, and in the process, both capture value. In a sense, the provider and the client co-produce the service event, because one can't do without the other. It stands to reason that the roles of

the client and the provider are different. In a doctor/patient service event, for example, the physician brings knowledge, time, and the necessary infrastructure. The patient brings him or herself, a medical history, and a perceived situation that requires attention. During the service process, the participants exchange information in various forms, resulting in a change to the people involved. The doctor's experience level and assets change, as do the patient's information level and physical or mental condition. There is more to it, of course, but this is the basic idea.

SERVICE – A PROFESSIONAL DIMENSION

In business, the case is slightly different. Some companies, such as professional firms, are totally service oriented. Other service companies, such as airlines and restaurants, have more complicated arrangements. An airline company, for example, could contract out its telephone service to another company, perhaps in another country, called *outsourcing*. In this scenario, agreements, specifying responsibilities and expectations, are required in most cases, to enhance the benefits to both parties.

In government, services are governed by convention and law. Constituents use governmental resources for information and a variety of physical services. In many cases, it is difficult to tell who is providing the service and who is receiving it.

In education, the provider/client relationship can be complex. Who is the provider and who is the client? Let's assume that the teacher provides the service to the student, by giving lectures and

managing classroom activity. But it could be more complicated than that. Consider a university setting. Does the professor provide a service to the administration by teaching courses and doing the myriad of other things faculty do? But then again, one could look at it the other way around by contending that the purpose of the administration is to provide the educational infrastructure. So the teacher could be a provider of services and a client of services, at the same time. We will take a look at complex service arrangements in follow-on sections of this chapter and in later chapters.

Returning to the airline example, let's assume that an agreement is made with a company in another country to run a call center whereby passengers can make reservations and obtain information. Ostensibly, the objective is to save money, improve the bottom line, and help the top management look good to the shareholders. The airline is the client and the call center company is the provider. How does the client (that is the airline company, in this case), who is a stakeholder with something to gain or lose, effectively control the situation? They collectively draw up a *service level agreement* that governs the quality of service, the number of calls to be handled in a specified period of time, the duration of the agreement, and the costs involved. Why don't the patient and the doctor have a service level agreement? They do, but it is implicit in the social setting in which medical services are performed.

There is another twist to the airline example. Where do you and I – the passengers – fit in? Again, the call center operator

provides an airline related service to us and we are the clients, even though we are, in fact, the provider of the financial resources that make the whole process work. The call center company effectively has two clients: the airline at the macro level and the set of passengers at the micro level.

It is commonplace for services to exist on two or more levels, as demonstrated by the airline example, in a service arrangement called a *service package*. In a service package, services are performed at differing levels and the service level agreement must reflect that eventuality. When a collection of service processes exist and they are all performed at the same level, it is called a *service bundle*. So if you go to a medical facility comprised of a team of doctors that essentially perform the same kinds of things, the set of service events is a service bundle. It follows in the case of the airline, that the service package contains a service bundle consisting of a group of telephone operators that provide services to passengers.

BUSINESS SERVICES

Some firms further complicate the picture by essentially being in two related service businesses at the same time. Consider an information technology (IT) company that provides services in two forms: consulting and outsourcing. With consulting, the firm tells a client how to do something, and with outsourcing, the firm does it for the client. As an example, the IT firm could advise on what information systems the client needs and then develop those systems. Similarly, it could provide information on how to set up an IT operation and then run that shop after it is set up.

Related to IT services is a general class of activities known as *business services*. With business services, like IT services, there are two options: consulting and outsourcing. With business service consulting, organizations are advised about business function, such as customer relationship management (CRM) and enterprise resource planning (ERP). Then, with outsourcing, the business services firm does it for you – perhaps in the areas of finance and accounting.

What we have at this point are multiple organizations, collections of people and technology connected by value propositions and shared information, operating as a service system. More specifically, a *service system* is defined as a configuration of people and technology connected to another system of people and technology in order to co-create value for both organizations.

DIFFERENCES BETWEEN PRODUCTS AND SERVICES

It is useful to consider the differences between products and services. Products are tangible and services are intangible. Now that is a pretty general statement. An automobile, a garment, a table, and even a fast-food hamburger are examples of products. A doctor's visit, swimming pool cleaning, and package delivery are examples of services. On the surface, one could conclude that products are produced through some relevant sequence of operations, but that is not a defining characteristic, since most services also go through a sequence of steps. The answer is that a

product is an artifact – something you can see or touch. Clearly, a service results in something worthwhile – otherwise, why engage in it – but the result is a change in a person or possession, not in the creation of something.

Products are storable; services are non-storable. You can store any of the examples of products, given above. If you have your car cleaned or your lawn mowed, you can't exactly save that service. When a service is finished, it is done forever. Perhaps, a record of the service is archived, explicitly or implicitly, but once the stop button is pushed, that service machine is off. If a service has to be repeated, then it is another service event.

Another related difference is that services are generally regarded as perishable. The implication here is that if a seat on an airline flight is not used, then the value of that opportunity is lost. There are many parallels between services and events in everyday life. If you buy a fresh banana and don't eat it within a reasonable time period, its value is lost. You can buy another, but again, that is a different thing.

With products, consumption follows production. In fact, the build-store-sell and the sell-build-ship business models apply here. With services, consumption and production occur at the same time. This characteristic is related to the difference between product quality and service quality. With products, a quality assessment can be made before the customer enters the scene. With services, the client's view of quality is determined during the service process.

As product classes mature, they become standardized and competition shifts to price. Services are almost always customized. In general, product development is capital intensive, and the delivery of services is labor intensive.

It is important to recognize, however, that the creation of products may include services in the production process, and that services may also accompany production in the form of follow-on activity.

CLASSIFICATION OF SERVICES

Given that services are pervasive in modern economies, there would appear to be so much diversity between them that it would be impossible to make any sense of the subject. After all, there does not seem to be much similarity between a lawn mowing operation and a service package for an airline – as simple examples. On the other hand, there has to be a set of common denominators that we could use to classify services so that we could draw some conclusions about organization, performance, and quality. After all, most of us would agree that clients would like to get the most for their money and providers would like to receive the greatest return on their investment of knowledge, time, and effort.

Service Criteria

Services are generally classified by at least five criteria, although one criterion dominates. The minor factors are degree of provider labor intensity, degree of customer interaction, level

of provider knowledge, and the amount of client information, that are quantitative measures brought to a service event. The major factor is a qualitative attribute known as "service nature," consisting of a service object and a service result. We will also identify other factors in the second chapter and refine the material given here when we establish a set of comprehensive service models. We will focus on the service object in this chapter, because it reflects whether a service is performed on a person, a possession, or information. In a previous section, we covered the subject of distinguishing services from goods. The service object is useful for distinguishing one service from another service, and it preserves the roles of the provider and the client. In a generic sense, the provider does the work and the client pays for it, and the question of who or what gets the service is the determining factor in exactly how much of the other four quantitative criteria are applied to a particular service event.

People Processing Services

In people processing services, the provider performs corporeal actions to the client. The client is part of the service production process and remains in the domain of the provider during service delivery. There is simultaneity of production with consumption in a people processing service event, and the provider and client, are regarded as co-producing the service. A trip to the dentist typifies this type of service, as does a reservation made through an airline call center. A people processing service can change either the physical state of a person, the mental state of a person, or both.

The physical state is something like increased fitness, manicured finger nails, or the location of a person. The mental state deals with non-physical attributes, such as increased knowledge, mental capability, or mental agility. Many people processing services do both, as in medical services and sports coaching.

Possession Processing Services

In possession processing services, the provider changes the state of one or more tangible objects under the jurisdiction of the client. Many possession processing services are straightforward, as in car washing and other maintenance activities. These services relate to the condition of an object and are regarded as physical services. Clearly, there are other attributes of service objects and one of the most common is ownership that puts retailing into the domain of service processing. In fact, some manufacturing operations consist of a sequence of services applied to a physical object or system. Another physical attribute is location, and an operation that provides components to a just-in-time production process is a form of service.

Information Processing Services

Information processing services deal with the collection, manipulation, interpretation, and transmission of data to create value for the client. Accounting, banking, consulting, education, insurance, legal, and news are commonly experienced examples of information processing services. There are important issues with information processing services, such as representation (as

with lawyers and accountants), infrastructure (as with computers, databases, and the Internet), and self-service (as with online facilities, ATM machines, and other administrative functions). This type of service is covered in a separate chapter, later in the book.

CHARACTERISTICS OF SERVICES

In spite of the prevalence of services in everyday life, the subject is rarely considered and seldom defined. In business, services are commonly referred to as the non-material equivalent of a good. Services can be sold, purchased, and scheduled. To many people, a service represents something they cannot do themselves or do not want to do, or perhaps more importantly, something that can be done more efficiently or in a less costly manner by a specialized business entity. In fact, the agricultural and manufacturing sectors of the economy employ services, and the service sector also uses services. That said, exactly what constitutes a service is still up in the air, and a summary of the major definitive characteristics is certainly in order.

> *A service is a process.* This notion is paramount to recognizing the far-reaching importance of service science as an academic discipline. A service takes input and produces output. In between the input and the output, there exist one or more steps that constitute the service process. Consider a simple medical example. A patient – the client – perceives a situation that requires attention. A

contact with a medical provider is made and an appointment is scheduled for a service event. In general, the following three items of information are brought to the service process: the patient per se, a medical history, and the relevant information for the current problem. This is the client/customer input required for a service process. The physician performs the requisite consultation, diagnosis, and resolution that collectively constitute the service process. The output then consists of the diagnosis, prescription, prognosis, and update of the medical records. Additionally, the personal knowledge bases of the patient and physician are enhanced as a result of the service event.

A service is heterogeneous. This characteristic reflects the fact that each client/provider interaction in the form of a service event is unique. Some researchers refer to this characteristic as the fact that services are customized, either by design or by happenstance. Each service query to an information system or each instance of personal service, for example, is inherently different.

A service captures value. A service event creates a benefit to both the client and the provider, in the form of a change of state that is reflected in their physical condition or location, a change in their possessions, or in their assets. A service provider

brings one or more of the following elements to the table: specific knowledge of the problem and solution domains, the time necessary to perform the service event, the physical wherewithal to perform the service event, and the requisite tools and equipment to perform the service event. Note that a location or infrastructure is not required since it may be associated with the client. The client provides the service object (i.e., the object or entity to which the service is applied) and necessary information, as required. The provider captures value through the execution of the service process. The client captures value as a result of the service process.

A service cannot be inventoried. The notion of opportunity loss is fundamental to service science. An empty seat on an airline flight cannot be resold. The value lost to a service provider due to a missed appointment cannot be regained. This characteristic gives a time dimension to services. Clearly, there are other flights and other appointments, but the time assigned to the execution of a service process is lost forever once the service window has closed. Thus, a service capacity is said to be *perishable*, referring to the fact that it is "perished" when unused.

A service is intangible. Although this characteristic was alluded to above, it deserves special attention because the definition of service products by the government uses the notion of a "change in the condition of a person or object" as the basis for classification. Services, especially in the areas of education and government, often result in social goods that are expressed in economic terms as hidden costs or opportunity costs.

A service is consumed at the point of production. This characteristic adds specificity to the recognition that a service is a process, even though it may be summarized for descriptive purposes as a service event. When a service terminates, it is finished. After the final step in a service process, the event is archived along with the consequent change of states of the client and provider.

A service cannot be resold or given away. It is not possible to pass a service on to another economic entity. The result of a service event is unique to that event, although information gained during the service process could theoretically be used by another entity. However, information resulting from a service event is not the same as the service event, because of the consumption characteristic.

A service is co-produced. This characteristic emphasizes the fact that because of the simultaneity of client and provider participation and the fact that a service event does not result in the production of a good, but rather in the state of something, it is commonly referred to as the co-production of value in the sense that if either of the participants were not present for the service event, it could not be interpreted as being a service.

An interesting question remains. Do the above characteristics uniquely reflect that a service is a process? There are two conditions: necessity and sufficiency. If a service process must possess a characteristic to be classified as a service, then that characteristic is a necessary condition. However, possessing a necessary characteristic does not guarantee that the entity involved is a service, because there may be other such characteristics. On the other hand, if a process possessing a given characteristic is thereby automatically classified as a service, then it is regarded as a sufficient condition.

SUMMARY

The subject of services is important to most people because they are employed in services and are also consumers of services. In the year 2000, U.S. service employment comprised 80% of the workforce. Surprisingly, very little attention is given to the service sector, in spite of the fact that most of us work in it.

A *service* is a provider/client interaction that creates and captures value. A unique characteristic of services, unlike agriculture and manufacturing, is that both parties participate in the transaction, and in the process, both capture value. In a sense, the provider and the client co-produce the service event, because one can't do without the other.

Services are generally classified by at least five criteria, although one criterion dominates. The minor factors are degree of provider labor intensity, degree of customer interaction, level of provider knowledge, and the amount of client information, that are quantitative measures brought to a service event. The major factor is a qualitative attribute known as "service nature," consisting of a service object and a service result. The focus is on the service object in this chapter, because it reflects whether a service is performed on a person, a possession, or information.

There are several definitive characteristics of services. They are summarized as follows. A service is a process. A service is heterogeneous. A service captures value. A service cannot be inventoried. A service is intangible. A service is consumed at the point of production. A service cannot be resold or given away. And finally, a service is co-produced.

SELECTED READING

Friedman, T.L., *The Lexus and the Olive Tree*, New York: Anchor Books, 2000.

Friedman, T.L., *The World is Flat: A Brief History of the Twenty-First Century*, New York: Farrar, Straus and Giraux, 2006.

Harvard Business Review, *Business Value of IT*, Boston: Harvard Business School Press, 1999.

IBM Almaden Services Research, "SSME: What are services?" http://almaden.ibm.com/ssme, 2006.

Katzan, H., *A View of Service Science*, Southeast Decision Science Institute, Savannah, GA, February 21-23, 2007.

Maglio, P. and J. Zysman, *Toward a Science of Service Systems*, Sofcon 2007, Carnegie Mellon University, April 30, 2007, pp. 5-6.

Malone, T., *The Future of Work*, Boston: Harvard Business School Press, 2004.

Sampson, S.E. and C.M. Froehle, "Foundations and Implications of a Proposed Unified Services Theory," *Production and Operations Management*, Vol. 15, No. 2 (Summer, 2006), pp. 329-343.

CHAPTER 9

Service Systems

———————————— ⟶⟵ ————————————

A *service system* is a collection of resources and economic entities, capable of engaging in or supporting one or more service events. The resources are the infrastructure and other facilities necessary to support the service process. The economic entities are the service provider and service client that co-produce the service event. In the case of a people processing service, the two economic entities, the service provider and the service client, have a single service relationship. In the case of possession processing services, the service environment would also consist of one or more tangible objects that serve as the service object of the service process. In this sense, the service object is referred to as the "*operand* of the service process." There are three relationships: one between the provider and client, one between the provider and service object, and an ownership relationship between the client and the service object. In most cases, a service system is required to sustain a service event of this nature. In this instance, the service target could be a possession of the client or an individual or an organizational entity over which the client has responsibility.

SYSTEMS CONCEPTS

In its most general sense, a *system* is a set of objects with relationships between the objects and between their attributes.

The objects are the components or parts of the system and are generally unlimited in scope and variety. In actual practice, however, the objects of which a system is synthesized give the system its structure, and implicitly determine the practical limits on its functional operability. Attributes are the properties of objects, and the relationships connect the system together, so it can be regarded as a single entity.

Relationships

A relationship can take the form of a physical connection, a logical similarity, a causal rule, and so forth. In a service system, a relationship is the service that the provider and the client co-produce. Neither a provider nor a client, by itself, is a service system. By definition, both entities are required, along with the relationship that takes the form of a service process.

Environment

Systems usually exist with the support of an environment. The *environment* of a system exists as the objects outside of a system. The attributes of the outside objects determine whether the operation of the system is affected by those objects, or the outside objects are changed by the operation of the system.

System Attributes

Open systems interface or exchange information with their environment; *closed systems* do not interface with their environment

and there is no exchange between them. In the same manner that objects possess attributes, systems do also. Systems have been variously classed as being adaptive, probabilistic, deterministic, stable, and possessing a feedback mechanism. Service systems are almost always open systems because they require a nurturing environment in order to survive.

Service Systems Ontology

The nature of the existence of a class of systems is referred to as a *systems ontology*, which establishes a distinction between real systems, conceptual systems, and abstract systems. The existence of *real systems* can be perceived or inferred by observation and exist independently of the observer. *Conceptual systems* utilize logical or mathematical constructs to model a system's operation. *Abstract systems* form a subset of conceptual systems and exist as conceptual systems with a real counterpart.

Service systems are real systems that are socially constructed, so that an appropriate ontology is encompassed by the following definition:

> The subject of *ontology* is the study of the *categories* of things that exist or may exist in some domain. The product of such a study, also called ontology, is a catalog of the types of things that are assumed to exist in a domain of interest *D* from the perspective of a person who uses the language *L* for the purpose of talking about *D*.

The types in the ontology represent the *predicates,* *word senses,* or *concept and relation types* of the language *L* when used to discuss topics in the domain *D.* (Sowa, 2000)

One common approach to the listing of ontological elements is to divide the entities into groups called *categories.* Each category is different from the others and has a descriptive of its own. It is in this latter sense that the service models, covered in chapter eight, serve as a basis for service systems.

Reductionist View

In order to have a service, you need three basic things: a client, a provider, and a service process. Each is required to materialize a service event. You can have all the service providers in the world, but without a client and a relationship, there is no service. The same holds true for clients and relationships. Accordingly, a provider without a client and an appropriate service relationship is viewed as a nascent provider, or perhaps an unrealized provider.

However, there is much more to a service system. In the next section, we concentrate on the infrastructure needed for the service. In later sections, we will focus on the service process.

SERVICE PROVISIONING

If a service provider and client can co-produce a service event, there must be some degree of geographical locality to the situation,

in the sense that the client travels to the provider or the provider travels to the client or the client and provider execute the service event in a third-party location or they communicate via some form of interactive device and its corresponding media. In other words, they have to get together.

The Service Facility

First of all, let's consider the case where the customer travels to facilities associated with the provider, such as an airline terminal, hospital, restaurant, retail establishment, or hotel – to name only a few examples. Furthermore, let's refer to the provider facilities as the *service factory*. The basic idea is that the customer remains at the service factory during service delivery.

The situation quickly gets complicated because it depends on whether or not the service is associated with a tangible object, an intangible object, or a production supply chain. A *pure service* is a service not associated with tangible objects, such as in medical treatment, hair coloring, and personal transportation. The service event is scheduled, initiated, terminated, and archived – all in the service factory. Many service processes are comprised of several steps called the *service chain*. Other services, not just pure services, consist of a service chain, but this characteristic is normally associated with pure services. When a service process consists of a service chain, it is said to be "scripted." Clearly, a service script may be implicit in the service, such as a doctor's visit, or it may be explicitly prescribed as part of a formal service agreement. Depending upon the complexity of the situation, services can

also be a part of a goods production process or a conventional supply chain.

The notion of a service factory also applies to service events in which the client picks up a tangible object, or receives an object resulting from a production process, as when an airline ticket is purchased at an airline terminal. So, for example, a drive-up window at a fast food restaurant is categorized as a service factory, since the client is physically located at the service facility however short the time span of the service event. In this case, however, the pick-up service is associated with a production process that engenders the associated tangible object. The client obtains an object that is closely associated with the pick-up service, in contradistinction to the case, as covered in the next section, where the client brings in some artifact to a service shop for service and later picks it up.

A related consideration is whether the service is classified as being discrete or continuous. Hospital service is continuous, consisting of a series of service events. Moreover, the service events may be dynamic in the sense that they are not necessarily planned beforehand. A doctor's visit, on the other hand, ordinarily consists of a service chain of planned events, wherein the services might include check in, get weighed, interact with the physician, and so forth.

Some continuous services, such as insurance and banking, incorporate a service factory that is closely associated with the provider but not the client. Clearly, services of this type have a

service initiation, service agreements, and eventually a termination; but in-between service events are dynamic in the sense that they may occur on an unscheduled and unplanned basis.

Still other services in this category may utilize more than one service facility, such as a check-in terminal and a transportation vehicle. However, the classification applies since the client occupies provider facilities for the duration of the service. Branch banking is a form of continuous service with more than one service facility

The Service Shop

Secondly, some services involve leaving a possession of the client at a service shop for later pick-up, as in the cases of dry cleaning and auto repair. Clearly, the service shop is associated with the service provider, and it is the service object, owned by the client, that occupies physical space in the service facility for the duration of the service process.

The Service Portal

Lastly, some services engage a virtual service facility for the duration of the service event. All of this sounds like the Internet, and that's the idea. However, the category also includes telecommuting and a variety of online and telephone services. In fact, any activity, generally classed as e-Commerce, falls under the umbrella of a service portal. Included in the category of service portals are a variety of information services and "do it yourself" activities.

An interesting phenomenon exists concerning the metaphorical conception of the World Wide Web (WWW). Maglio and Matlock (Maglio and Matlock, 1998) interviewed beginning and experienced web users and determined that people naturally think of the web as a physical space in which they move. So, even though the web is not physical, users – that is, clients in the service domain – conceptually travel to the service provider.

Mobile Service Facilities

In the previous categories, the emphasis has been on provider resources that occupy a fixed space, incorporating personnel, buildings, equipment, machines, vehicles, and supplies. The scenario has been that the client travels to the service facility or accesses it via some modern convenience. There are also services wherein the provider travels to a third party location to perform a service for a client, such as car washing. In this form of service, the provider travels to a location, such as a parking lot, where the service is performed. Various forms of road service additionally fall into this category.

In other cases, the client moves, as in navigation services and various forms of satellite communication, such as radio, information providing, and related services – such as car unlocking.

Client Facilities

The subject of service provisioning would not be complete without the mention of client facilities, as in the case where the service provider travels to the client to perform a service, such as personal training, lawn care, cleaning, landscaping, and so forth. In most instances in this group, the service is performed on a possession of the client – even though that is not a necessary condition.

SERVICE IMPLEMENTATION

All organizations and all persons do not have the same service requirements and accordingly, the same problems. Moreover, it is impossible to look at services from solely an industry perspective or even a personal point of view. Clearly, services differ between industries and between persons. On the other hand, the diverse set of activities universally called *services* wouldn't be called *services* if there weren't some degree of commonality among them. Accordingly, we are going to take a look at steps in the service process, not necessarily service interactions, per se, that are commonly incorporated into the service chain. Next, we will take a look at operations that are specific to a particular service.

Generic Functions Performed During Service

It is necessary and important to emphasize the difference between generic functions performed to sustain a service – any service – and specific operations performed to achieve a particular

service. In the former case, we are dealing with steps that support a service process including: initiation, entry administration, sustaining service interactions, termination, exit administration, and archiving. Some of the functions are not present in all services, or they are implicit in an informal service arrangement. In most cases, the generic functions necessary for sustaining services can be viewed as organizational activities.

Service *initiation* refers to the steps necessary to schedule a service and establish a provider/client interaction. Appointments with professional service providers are normally scheduled, whereas arrangements with nonprofessionals are commonly scheduled on an informal basis. Some service providers use appointments to manage demand as a means of achieving service efficiency. Entry service *administration* initiates customer input, such as filling out forms, and establishes a service agreement encompassing fees and expectations. Legal documents may be involved with this step, and client requirements are delineated. Service *interactions* are the steps in the service process. For discrete service processes, service interactions are statically planned with expected variations, since most services are customized by the provider for each client. For continuous service processes, service interactions are dynamically engaged – as in the case of banking, insurance, and hospital care. Service *termination* represents the end of a set of service interactions, regardless if they are statically or dynamically executed. Follow-on services or referrals are established during this step. Exit service *administration* initiates the record-keeping process and deals with the economic aspects of

the service process. Service *archiving* handles information storage and legal requirements.

Collectively, the six generic functions are normally present, explicitly or implicitly, in practically all service processes, and are referred to as the *service platform*. The intended meaning of the terminology is that the service platform supports the service process.

Generic Operations Performed to Achieve Service

Most, if not all, operations performed in a service environment can easily be mapped to the seven generic operations given. *Scheduling* refers to demand management. *Customer input* represents the collaboration and information exchange portion of a service event. The entry identified as "perform services" is the subset of the service chain peculiar to a particular form of service. *Referral* is the stage in some forms of consultation where the client is directed to another service provider for more definitive service. *Representation* denotes a step in the service chain where the service provider, or an associate, represents the client in some form of negotiation. Two noteworthy examples of representation are in legal or tax service. *Auxiliary services* represent tasks performed to support the primary service function, such as taking blood for a physical examination. *Supplementary services* are activities such as billing, financing, and reporting – operations that are not directly part of the primary service function. A couple of examples will demonstrate this point of view.

The traditional operations performed in banking are teller activity, check clearing, transaction processing, record keeping, vault operations, treasury operations, security, and maintenance. Teller activity, transaction processing, and record keeping are associated with scheduling, customer input, and service performance. The other banking operations, customarily known as back-office operations easily map to supplementary and auxiliary service.

Another example is airline service. The traditional airline functions are customer support and ticketing, ground support, ground operations, and flight operations that easily correspond to scheduling, customer input, service performance, and auxiliary operations.

Traditional law office operations present a good example of diversity, since the commonly known operations of scheduling, consultation, research, reporting and representation readily correspond to the given generic operations.

BUSINESS SERVICE SYSTEMS

The basis of business service systems is the evolution from collaboration to automation. The first phase, entitled *Collaboration*, utilizes human engineering principles and is characterized as "assistance by doing some of the work." The next phase, entitled *Augmentation*, utilizes technology to increase productivity by using tools to supplement human activity. The third phase, entitled *Delegation*, is the outsourcing to service providers of non-core

business processes that do not provide competitive advantage. The final phase, entitled *Automation*, employs technology to provide self-service systems. Employing the four elements of business service systems, namely organization, technology, management, and information systems, service businesses can move among the phases by considering the following elements: business value (*Should we?*), technology (*Can we?*), governance (*May we?*), and business priorities (*Will we?*).

Globalization

A business service system is a complex socio-techno-economic system that combines people, technology, value, and clients along four dimensions: information sharing, work sharing, risk sharing, and goods sharing. (Maglio and Spohrer, 2007), There is some evidence that some elements of all four dimensions are present in all business service systems. Before globalization, services were performed between provider and client with some degree of locality. After Globalization Three (Friedman, 2006), business value creation through services is created by sharing. Information and communications technology (ICT) is the key business driver in value creation, and is the form of technology most closely aligned with business service systems.

Information and Communications Technology

ICT is the latest in a long chain of buzzwords intended to refer to what business, government, and education do with computers. The most interesting implication of the acronym ICT, however, is

that the availability of computers and communications to do just about any digital job we can think of is taken for granted. In a real sense, it is the application of technology to the co-creation of value by the interaction of provider and client, without requiring that the service participants be in the same location.

An information system is a collection of hardware, software, databases, telecommunications facilities, people, and operational procedures designed to collect, manipulate, store, process, and communicate data among components of an enterprise. An information system, sometimes known as a computer-based information system, is a service provider and its clients are the people, employees, business partners, and even other information systems in that application domain. As a multidimensional service provider, an information system is a platform for the nationalization and globalization of services. The effect of ICT is not restricted to information alone. Through ICT, multinational supply chains, to give only one example, are not only possible, but desirable.

The effectiveness of ICT is, of course, directly related to the Internet, because it lowers the cost of operating on a national and international scale. Consumers and enterprises alike can operate in a global marketplace to obtain lower costs for goods and services on a 24/7 schedule. Clearly, low-cost suppliers and service providers are available globally. The use of ICT in service provisioning is more closely associated with business services than it is with personal and domestic services.

Business Agility

Businesses operating digitally through ICT can leverage time and space globally to better respond to market demands. An agile firm is one that achieves responsiveness by allowing work to proceed continuously (*time management*) and at multiple international locations (*space management*).

Outsourcing

Outsourcing is the transfer of the ownership of a business process to a supplier, which includes management and day-to-day execution of that function (Wikipedia, 2007). The most commonly outsourced business processes are information technology, human resources, accounting, customer support, and call center operations. The key characteristics of outsourcing are "transfer" and ownership; it is different from the process in which the buyer retains control and tells the supplier how to do the work. The objective of outsourcing can be and often is one of the following: reducing costs, focusing the capability of a particular business on more profitable activities, and obtaining special capabilities that the provider firm may possess. Core business competencies are usually not outsourced. For example, airlines commonly outsource telephone reservation and information systems to foreign companies in order to reduce costs and focus on flight operations. Another example, more close to home, is the outsourcing of business cleaning services to benefit from economies of scale for that type of service.

With outsourcing, the client and the provider enter into a business relationship, established with a substantial business agreement, and then the service provider takes over the business process. Outsourcing is usually – actually, almost always – associated with offshoring, but that need not necessarily be the case.

Offshoring

Offshoring is a general term that describes the relocation of a business process from one country to another (Wikipedia, 2007). Although the present context is services, the practice also applies to manufacturing and production. If a country can provide services in a less expensive manner than other countries, it gives them a comparative advantage to freely trade those services. In the modern world of ICT for the appropriate services, therefore, offshoring can be achieved by establishing the necessary business ecosystem.

To be more specific, offshoring is the practice of transferring an internal business process of a company in one country to another country, to be executed by the same or a different company. Service offshoring is particularly appealing to modern business since many services can be digitized thereby facilitating inter-country relocation.

Offshoring may involve the transfer of intellectual property and training to the receiving country and is related to the availability of educated and trained labor as factors in production – the others

being land and capital. According, many design and development services have been redirected offshore.

Outsourcing and Offshoring

It follows from the above discussion that a company that engages in the transfer of an entire business function to another company in another country is both outsourcing and offshoring. As mentioned previously, common examples of outsourcing are call centers, accounting, customer support, human relations, and information technology (IT). It is now appropriate to add medical diagnosis, design services, and engineering services to the list and recognize that both outsourcing and offshoring are involved.

Public opinion on combined outsourcing and offshoring (O&O) is negative, because it is generally felt that the process adversely affects individuals and the total labor market. Even in cases in which O&O is associated with lower jobless rates, it is felt that O&O tends to shift displaced workers into lower paying jobs.

Transformational Outsourcing

Many executives feel that outsourcing allows the firm to concentrate on core competencies and, in the case of ICT, achieve greater flexibility. Because many business processes are totally dependent upon computers, business agility is necessary for developing responsiveness in the marketplace. *Transformational outsourcing* refers to the combination of cost saving with the

potential for strategic flexibility and supplements cost focus with opportunity focus.

The underlying idea is that through transformational outsourcing, the firm will be transformed into one with the requisite characteristics. Innovation in supplying services is required, therefore, because services are almost always customized and are labor intensive. Moreover, competition in the services marketplace does not tend to drive down process and profit margins.

The key point, of course, is that outsourced services do not usually provide differentiation in the marketplace.

Sharing

The major tenet of services is that the provider and the client co-produce a service event and the composite interaction creates value for both of the participants. To a greater or lesser degree, a service is enacted by sharing, as covered previously (Maglio and Spohrer, 2007). Information sharing is more closely aligned with services in which persons interact, such as medical provisioning and consulting. Work sharing is characterized by outsourcing. Risk sharing (although not covered so far) is associated with continuous form of service, such as insurance, and is related to transformational outsourcing. Goods sharing is involved with certain formal tangible people-oriented services, such as hotel and auto rental.

Composite Services

It is conceivable that a firm will want to transfer certain in-house operations to another country to reduce costs and take advantage of specific labor conditions. This process, sometimes known as FDI, or Foreign Direct Investment, allows the firm to maintain control while achieving the aforementioned benefits. From that point, it is a short step from inside offshoring to outside offshoring.

Another outsourcing possibility is to transfer equipment and personnel to the supplier, along with the business process, as in the case of some companies that transferred their total ICT operations to an outside company. Many people feel, however, that the transferred personnel have a lower level of job security in their new employment habitat.

Finally, chapter one covered the case where services exist at two or more levels, as in the airline example. In this example, the outsourced and offshored service company enters into a service agreement with the airline to deliver information and reservation services to passengers. In this instance, the service provider has two clients: the airline and the passengers, with no stake in the eventual outcome except as governed in the service level agreement. Service packages in this category have serious drawbacks in the area of service quality and customer retention.

SERVICE PROCESS ORGANIZATION

Practically everyone has heard of or experienced service providers that traditionally have clients backed up with very long waiting times. Another common example is the "not so fast" fast-food restaurant. In the world of services, organization is everything.

Expectations

While it is literally impossible to solve all service problems in a few pages, it is feasible to deliver an organizational design that is relevant to most service systems. Recall the definition of a service system that reads, "A *service system* is a system of people and technology that adapts to the changing value of information is the system." It is important to emphasize that the "changing value of information" also refers to the service process itself. In other words, know thyself. So it should be expected that a particular service organization would adjust to changing conditions in the workplace.

In the production of goods, a measure of organization is the level of inventory, even though the management of inventory can be a subject in its own right. With services, capacity is key, and long waiting lines are evidence of insufficient service capacity, ineffective demand management, or inadequate organization.

In this section, a working model of service organization is presented that should serve as a starting point for looking at organizational issues.

An Organization Example – Retailing and Services

The importance of service organization is inherent in retailing. Retailing is a service, as covered previously, and the sales service event changes the ownership attribute of a product. A significant aspect of retailing exists, however, that is associated with service organization.

There is a component in retailing that is directly related to the level of expected service as a function of the price of the product. Most customers possess a nominal price for a given product. If the sales price is lower than nominal value, then less service is expected. If the sales price is higher than the nominal price, then more service is expected or the product is deemed overpriced. Buyer behavior, therefore, is governed by a combination of price and retail service, so that buyer behavior is influenced to some degree by service organization.

Service, Service Providers, and Service Process

Clearly, there is a difference between a service and its service provider. In doctoring, the service is the medical attention afforded the patient, and the service provider is the doctor. In auto maintenance and repair, the service provider is the dealership (assuming new car sales, adhering to the KISS principle) and

the service process is the well-known service event, involving the service advisor, service technician, and a whole host of other providers.

Accordingly, the *service process* is the following set of steps in the service chain, mentioned previously: service initiation, entry administration, service interactions, service termination, and service archiving. This is a generic set of steps, and each particular form of service has its own set of provisional operations. We will develop a service organization model based on the given generic service chain.

Transitional Service Organization Model

In a transitional form of service organization, the service process from the client's and service provider's viewpoints consists of the following steps. (1) The owner (client) makes an appointment for service with the appointment scheduler (the demand manager). (2) The client brings the car (service object) to the dealership for service. (3) The client interacts with the service advisor (service facilitator) to exchange service particulars. (4) The client waits for service or leaves the dealership's premises (the service factory). (5) The service arrangement is entered into a computer (the service scheduler) by the service facilitator. (6) The service technician (the server) subsequently picks up the service order and performs the required service, often coordinating with the service facilitator for additional information. (7) The server registers the service completion with the service scheduler. (8) The service scheduler sends a request to the service administrator for

billing. (9) The client interacts with the service administrator for pickup and payment resolution and the service event is completed.

The service model consists of five key relationships: governance, information, service, ownership, and the service-level agreement. Additionally, there are nine major components: the service provider, the service client, the service manager, the service facilitator, the service scheduler, the service server, the service object, the demand manager, and the service administrator. Each element is considered in detail in a subsequent chapter on the business of services.

The model applies to the three major forms of service: people processing, possession processing, and information services, as covered in the next chapter.

SUMMARY

A service system is a system of people and technology that adapts to the changing value of knowledge in the system. The participants in a service system are the provider and client, and the relationship between them is the service process. Systems of this type require an environment in which to operate that can take the form of a service factory in which the client resides for the duration of the service process and the service shop in which a possession of the client resides for the duration of the service event.

Service systems are facilitated by information and communications technology and enhanced by globalization. Service provisioning is inherent in outsourcing and offshoring. Innovation in supplying services is required because services are usually customized and labor intensive.

Core business processes are not customarily outsourced, and outsourcing predominantly does not provide differentiation in the marketplace. The transitional service organization model demonstrates the commonality and variability of service systems, and gives rise to three proposed laws of service systems.

SELECTED READING

Friedman, T.L. (2006), *The World is Flat: A Brief History of the Twenty-First Century*, New York: Farrar, Straus and Giraux.

Sowa, John F. (2000), *Knowledge Representation: Logical, Philosophical and Computational Foundations*, Brooks Cole Publishing, Pacific Grove Publishing, Inc.

Offshoring (2007). http://en.wikipedia.org/wiki/Offshoring.

Ontology (2007). http://en.wikipedia.org/wiki/Ontology.

Outsourcing (2007). http://en.wikipedia.org/wiki/Outsourcing.

Maglio, P.P. (2007), *Service Science, Management, and* Engineering (SSME)*: An Interdisciplinary Approach to Service Innovation*, IBM Almaden Research Center, http://almaden.ibm.com/ssme, p. 14.

IBM Almaden Services Research (2006), *Service Science, Management, and* Engineering (SSME)*: Challenges, Frameworks, and Call for Participation,* http://almaden.ibm.com/ssme, p. 13.

Maglio, P.P. and J. Spohrer (2007), *Fundamentals of Service Science,* IBM Almaden Research Center.

Maglio, P.P. and T. Matlock (1998), *Metaphors We Surf the Web By,* The Information Architecture Institute.

CHAPTER 10

Information Services

Through information and communications technology (ICT), modern society has made enormous advances in how we live and work. How far we have progressed is summarized by Microsoft chairman Bill Gates in a recent email message. "The ability to access and share information instantly and communicate in ways that transcend the boundaries of time and distance has given rise to an era of unprecedented productivity and innovation that has created new economic opportunities for hundreds of millions of people around the world and paved the way for global growth that is unparalleled in human history." (Gates, 2007)

INFORMATION SERVICE CONCEPTS

An *information service* is a resource capable of supporting a service event or instantiating a service event based on information. In other words, an information service can assist in the execution of a service, such as in retailing, or it can actually be the service as when buying a pair of shoes on the Internet – actually, the World Wide Web, but that distinction is not required at this point. The resource is a service provider that can take the form of a person or a computer. The execution of an information service event requires a service client that can also take the form of a person or computer, and the provider and client must interact in order to

co-produce the service. The execution of a service event changes the state of the provider and the client, but a tangible object is not produced. An information service is commonly associated with computer technology, but that is not a necessary condition. The most definitive characteristic of an information service is that the information travels, which gives rise to new models of information management and communications technology.

A Personal Dimension

Most of the information that is communicated between people is about something. When you buy a car, the sales person tells you about the key features and how to use them. In the physician/patient relationship, the doctor and patient exchange information about a medical situation. Clearly, there is some form of informational interchange that accompanies practically all services. Information service is more than the incidental exchange of information.

With information services, the client specifically requests information and the provider supplies it using some form of a communications channel. The service request may be implicit in another form of activity or it may be "ordered" on a demand basis, but it is nevertheless requested.

Data versus Information

Each provider/client interaction in an information service requires a context, and here is why. Pure unadulterated facts

are known as *data*. For example, the date April 15th can mean different things to different people. To many Americans, it means tax day. To others, it may be the start of the baseball season. To grandmother, it may be her birth date. *Information* is data in a particular context so it has a specific meaning.

When you request some information about a subject from an Internet web site, for example, the context is supplied implicitly or explicitly, such as from the site itself, the nature of the query, or even information in a previously requested web page. The context effectively gives meaning to data and turns it into information. The bits that flow through wires or through the air as electromagnetic radiation are nothing more than data, at best. Accordingly, it would be proper to say that it is an information service that turns a bunch of bits into something useful, such as a news story or downloaded music.

Ordinary Mail

Not all information services necessarily require a computer. The United States Postal Service is a case in point, as is its international equivalent known as the PTT (Post, Telephone, and Telegraph), which does not require a computer in its basic form. Electronic mail (email as we generally know it) is also an information service, and it does require a computer. Each element has a sender and an intended recipient.

Who is the service provider? It is certainly not the sender or recipient. Clearly, it is the mail service itself. If you're thinking

that the mail service is the communications channel, then you are on the right track. In this instance, and this instance only, the sender and receiver are the clients and the mail service is the service provider. In most other information services, the communications channel *is* only the channel for communication and nothing more. With mail service, pickup, transportation, and delivery would appear to be the service, and the informational content of the message is not brought into the analysis.

Is Software a Service?

Yes. Software would appear to be a service, such as in document preparation and as suggested by the example of ordinary mail. Information is moved from one place to another and perhaps it is transformed a bit in the process. In document preparation, or word processing, as it is usually called, information is moved from an origin, such as a person's brain, through the nervous system, the person's fingers, and the keyboard to the computer and software and then to a document file. Nevertheless, it is transferred from one place to another. If electronic mail is considered to be a service, then it would seem that word processing is also. Consider another example. If you go to a tax preparation agency to have your return prepared, you consider it to be a service. If you buy a program for a small fee that does the same work as the tax agency, does it perform a service? Most people would agree that tax software is a service. In the same vein, presentation, spreadsheet, and database software would also be regarded as services.

There is another aspect to all of this, as exemplified by the word processing and email examples. The provider and client participate in the exchange of information, even though they may not be, and probably won't be, in close proximity. Thus, the distance metric is not necessarily significant in word processing, and in the case of email, even the time metric is also not significant.

Is *all* software a service? Perhaps, that should have been the original question. It is an open item. It is easy to conceptualize that office software for document preparation, presentation, graphics, data management, and data analysis could be regarded as services, since that software facilitates the transfer of information from one place to another. In the area of information systems, DSS (Decision Support System) software, for example, provides timely information to managers to aid in decision making. DSS software is definitely a service. What about AI (Artificial Intelligence) software, such as software that monitors gauges in a nuclear reactor? Then, if something goes wrong, the computer program shuts the reactor down before a meltdown occurs. Again, most people, especially those that work in nuclear power plants, would agree that it is a service. The debate could go on. For this chapter, at least, software is a service.

Practically speaking, a software package, by itself, does not qualify to be an information service. In order to be functioning as a service, software must be operating on a computer in order to respond to a client's request in an appropriate manner. You always need a computer and communications infrastructure to support software services.

ENTERPRISE INFORMATION SERVICES

Information is the cornerstone of modern business, and government as well, and is the major ingredient in everyday commerce. In the study of information services, the distinction between information and the system to handle the information is often blurred. In this section, we will establish the difference between information and services.

"About" Information

A lot of information is about things: about a product or service, about travel arrangements, about how to do something, about a sporting event, about a person or group, about something that has happened in the past, and so forth. We are going to refer to this type of information as *operand information*, and we are additionally going to refer to information that is involved with the service process itself as *operant information*. When the focus of an information service is the result, then as Vargo and Lusch (Vargo and Lusch, 2004) might put it, we are using goods-dominant logic and the result is referred to as the operand. When the focus of an information service is on the process, then we are employing service-dominant logic and the operant resources are the information and the other steps in the service process.

Business Information

Business information services are usually divided into two categories: operational services and management services.

Operational services are employed to run the enterprise and management services are used to manage the enterprise. Some of the same basic concepts are used in both categories, but the time and distance characteristics are different. For example, a database management system and a database are normally used to store persistent data for the enterprise. With operational services, the database is dynamic and can be updated for each transaction. With management services, static data is needed to make effective decisions. Accordingly, a static database would ordinarily be created from the dynamic database so that timely management reports could be generated. Of course, this is a bit of a simplification, but the basic idea is there.

The management of information is an enterprise service in its own right. Clearly, the transfer of information from operational databases to a data warehouse for making decisions is a concrete example of an enterprise information service.

Transaction Services

When you make an airline reservation or check a flight schedule using the Internet, you are using a transaction processing system. You are actually using the World Wide Web, but this is a discussion for another section. If you are going to New York, for example, do you say, "I'm going by car" or do you say "I'm going by highway"? Do you fly by plane or by air? The level of specificity is important in information services. Most information services that support operational systems in today's world use transaction

processing, comprised of the following elements: client computer, communication channel, and server computer.

At the most general level, you interact with the server using the communications channel. You are the client, the server is the provider, and the service is the transaction. The communications channel between the passenger's computer and the server is probably the Internet. The second communications channel could be the Internet or a dedicated network. Some people call this channel the *service bus*; we will go into more detail on this subject shortly. The server computer is a client to the flight reservations computer, which is the service provider and whatever request the former makes to the latter is the service. In a similar vein, the database management system provides a service to the flight reservation computer. The entire process is mediated by hardware and software and the only thing that moves is the information.

Information Processing

Fundamental to all the modern-day hype about the Internet, social networking, and online collaboration is the much maligned subject of data processing, or as it is now called "information processing." In today's world of software development, there are no programmers – only software engineers. In the age of data processing, there were no programmers – only systems analysts. It is literally amazing how those 10 billion lines of COBOL code that run everyday business got written. COBOL stands for Common Business Oriented Language. *Information processing* is what computers do to sustain business operations and

comprise what we will refer to as the operant of the information service process. Information systems are the hardware, software, communications, organizational, and human facilities that sustain information processing. There are macro operations (as in macro economics) such as accessing records, sorting records, merging records, storing records, manipulating records, and reporting; and there are micro operations (again as in micro economics) such as reading, writing, moving, and performing arithmetic operations on specific pieces of data. Collectively, macro and micro operations are the substance of information services.

An effective information service requires effective information that is usually taken to mean that the information is timely, accurate, complete, relevant, accessible, verifiable, and reliable. The attributes of information determine the efficacy of an information service.

Client and Provider Input to an Information Service

An information service requires client and provider input, just as in any other kind of service. Usually, the client – whether it is a person or a computer – enters a small amount of information into the service process. The provider – usually a computer information system – has access to a larger store of information, so that we can say the provider provisionally supplies a larger amount of information. The informational output of an information service is a function of the inputs and the nature of the service.

The client may have help supplying input to an information service through hardware and software facilities known as "interaction services." The provider may have assistance from database services and auxiliary services via a service bus.

Interaction Services

Most people are familiar with user-friendly graphical user interfaces, known as GUIs. Desktop environments and web pages are common examples. An *interaction service* is a familiar idiom for interacting with a computer. Clearly, this is a client's point of view. An interaction service is normally a socially-constructed collection of structural elements and behavioral patterns, such as action buttons, list boxes, and pull-down menus. The idea is to get information into the computer in the most efficient manner, and there are two basic methods: a command-line interface and a GUI interface. The command-line interface demands textual input and is great for a wide range of technical environments. For most clients, a GUI interface is superior.

Interaction services are dependent upon what the client expects to do with the information service. Here are some examples:

- Information exploration (e.g., find out about service science)
- Accomplish something (e.g., reserve a seat)
- Find a "good enough" answer to a question (e.g., how do we get to New York?)

- Change the direction of a search operation (e.g., what about service systems?)
- Establish a point of reference (e.g., mark my place to come back to at a later time)

Designing effective interaction services is not so easy but one approach is to think about the elements with which you have to work. A common set of such elements is composed of objects (such as icons), actions (such as a file menu), subjects (such as the information that you have to work with), and tools (such as calendars and appointments).

Interaction services are a small part of service science, but nevertheless an important part.

Service Bus

A *service bus* is a high-speed data link between two computing platforms that operate in a request/response mode. The client requests an item of information (such as the price of IBM stock on Monday at 11:00 on a given date) and the provider, which operates in a server mode, supplies it in an expeditious manner. A service bus requires software that is called *middleware*.

An example of the need for a service bus is inherent in the following example. A stock broker is on a line to a client who requests the price of IBM stock. The brokerage firm has a computer (the server) that gets an up-to-the-second feed from the stock exchange. There is a high speed link between the stock

brokers and the server, and each broker has a specialized thick client interface. The broker enters the stock symbol for IBM into a text box and clicks a send button. The server responds in a fraction of a second with the requested price.

Collaboration

Teams are the accepted norm in the modern enterprise, and collaboration is the process by which they progress toward a common goal. With information services, collaboration between groups and individuals can be effected from geographically dispersed locations. In general, collaboration has a well-defined structure and set of operational procedures that employs any or all of four recursive information service modalities: email, instant messaging, interactive media, and specially designed collaborative software.

Collaboration operates at the intellectual level and often benefits from decentralization and varying degrees of academic and personal diversity. Collaboration is a unique form of service. The service provider in the information service modality is established through information and communications technology, and is an instance of where the "service is the service provider," because it allows the clients in a collaboration service to exchange meaningful information.

Collaboration requires at least two clients interacting in what is referred to as a *multiclient service*. A multiclient service is frequently leaderless and is known as a *virtual organization*

structure. Traditional workflow where a document is passed between team members is a common form of collaboration.

INFORMATION SERVICE APPLICATIONS

The range of information services is multidimensional. Information services are ubiquitous and touch on all aspects of everyday life. It would seem that everything affects everything, and the medium of exchange is information. Looking at the big picture, the four big players are people, business, education, and government. People interact with themselves and with business and government to engage in commerce, obtain information and services, and to participate in various forms of interpersonal communication. Businesses interact with people, other businesses, and the government to make a profit. The government interacts with other governmental entities, as well as people and businesses to provide a requisite level of service. The fuel that feeds the fire is information, which is sustained by the environment, technology, economics, and society. In the world of the Internet and the World Wide Web, information services are paramount.

Pull versus Push

It is perhaps a bit of an oversimplification, but "the manner in which you approach an information service determines what you get." The characteristics of the *pull model* are succinctly summarized in the following sentence. "Rather than 'push,' this new approach focuses on 'pull' – creating platforms that help people to mobilize appropriate resources when the need

arises." Hagel and Brown (2007) have identified the pull model as a means of establishing business resources for the upcoming generation of business activities based on mass communications and the Internet.

Push models are essentially scripted and thrive in stable environments with little uncertainty. Forecasting, as in demand forecasting, is key in push environments and allows high levels of efficiency to be developed in business processes. Most of modern business and governmental activity uses the push modality. A business pushes a product into the marketplace and people buy it. Push programs are top-down processes with the following steps: design, deploy, execute, monitor, and refine.

Pull models increase value creation for both clients and providers. For clients, "pull" activity expands the scope of available resources. For providers, pull systems expand the market for services. Pull platforms are associated with the following attributes: uncertain demand, emergent design, decentralized environment, loosely coupled modular construction of facilities, and on-demand service provisioning. Pull models are more amenable to uncertain business conditions.

From both the client's and the provider's perspectives, pull services focus on the following activities: find, select, purchase, deliver, and service. If all of this sounds familiar, it should be. It represents how you buy shoes on the Internet.

Enterprise Service Constituents

The seven constituents of an enterprise information service are providers, clients, messages, communications, information processing, persistent storage, and the user interface that collectively take into consideration the requisite technology including database facilities, email archives, protocols, business rules, operational procedures, and a variety of service interactions needed for enterprise applications. Since information, and not people, move in information services, this category of service is based on information and communications technology. It is important that when we discuss information services at the enterprise level, we are primarily concerned with functionality and not necessarily with computing platforms.

Information Service Model

Information service systems typically operate in a client/ server mode, which means that the end user is the service client, the enterprise application running on a computing platform is the service provider, and the means of client and provider interaction is some form of communications channel. Typically, the client enters information into the system through a well-defined interface and the provider does something in return. Exactly what the provider does is of primary importance to the information service system.

There are at least three distinct possibilities:

- The provider accesses some form of persistent storage and returns selected information to the client.
- The provider performs some element of information processing and returns an indicator to the client that it was done.
- The client and the provider enter into an interactive dialog concerning specific informational elements and a supply chain operation is initiated to accomplish the corresponding enterprise operation.

As such, information service systems are instrumental in supporting daily activities. Typical business applications are order processing, purchasing, accounting, inventory control, human resources, marketing and sales support, manufacturing, and various forms of service support including data collection and information management.

An *enterprise resource planning* (ERP) service is an integrated collection of constituent applications operating at the enterprise level that provide information services in six comprehensive areas: production, supply chain, customer relationship management, sales support and ordering, financial and managerial accounting, and human resources. An ERP service essentially operates by using a cross section of diverse traditional business applications to satisfy client requests for information and is particularly appropriate to a global environment. Customer relationship management (CRM) is frequently presented as a separate topic.

Scope of Electronic Information Services

It is possible to be more definitive about electronic information services. The three main constituents are business, government, and the consumer, and the main combinations are B2C, B2B, B2G, G2B, G2C, G2G, and C2C. B2C means business-to-consumer; B2B means business-to-business; B2G means business-to-government; G2B means government-to-business; G2C means government-to-consumer; G2G means government-to-government: and C2C means consumer-to-consumer. In the symbols, the leftmost letter reflects the provider and the rightmost letter represents the client.

Electronic Commerce

Electronic commerce is an enterprise information service application supported by the Internet and the World Wide Web, and can be viewed as an opportunistic means of doing business with minimal cost. In short, the information services of the Internet and the Web are used to conduct business.

Electronic commerce is usually known as e-commerce or B2C for short. Conventional business establishments are referred to as "brick and mortar" facilities characterized by a shopping area in which customers can view products, and business personnel can conduct commerce. The equivalent in the digital world is an e-commerce web site where a consumer can conduct analogous functions. The service provider is the e-commerce web site and the customer is the client connected to the web site via the Internet.

In this instance, the Internet is the communications channel. The service process is the set of interactions between the customer and one or more web sites that go through the following steps: find, select, purchase, deliver, and service.

Find is an Internet service process, which is usually a set of service interactions, to navigate to the desired Internet retailer. After the electronic retailer is chosen, the *select* and *purchase* services represent the online equivalent of the traditional processes of making a purchase. Purchasing involves payment that invokes a secure service designed for that specific purpose. *Deliver* is another service process initiated by the retailer for physically delivering the product to the consumer. *Service* is the web-enabled service process of providing customer support. Each of the steps in the B2C service process (i.e., find, select, purchase, deliver, and service) involves at least one service, so the entire process can be properly regarded as a *multiservice*, driven by a series of constituent information services.

B2C transactions are characterized by increased convenience, enhanced efficiency, additional buying choice, and lower prices, from the consumer's perspective, and by an increased return on retailing investment for the electronic retailer. An electronic retailer need not have a related "brick and mortar" facility, but that is often the case.

Electronic Business

Electronic business is the use of the Internet and the World Wide Web to conduct business operations, including intra-business and inter-business transactions. This is a broad category and ranges from relatively simple information services to obtain tacit business information from within a single organization to complex web services.

Electronic business is usually known as e-business or B2B for short and has its roots in electronic data interchange (EDI) commonly used to exchange information on business operations within an organization, and between business partners, suppliers, and wholesalers. The use of the Internet for communications services reduces operational costs for computer networks and increases the value obtained from costs that are incurred.

The major advantage of B2B operations is that companies can utilize an information service known as the "B2B Electronic Marketplace," wherein they can buy and sell products and exchange information through a *virtual marketplace*. Not only can companies create supply chains, but they can create business partnerships in which one company can take advantage of the information services of another company. The process, known as the *componentization of information services*, facilitates the creation of web services that allow the company to be a more responsive (to market and economic conditions) enterprise.

B2B is similar to B2C in one respect. Modern company operations require the purchase of certain *indirect materials*, typically referred to as MRO materials, where MRO stands for "maintenance, repair, and operations," and include such items as ball pens, repair parts, and office equipment. Through the B2B electronic marketplace, various companies can collectively achieve lower cost through *demand aggregation*.

Direct materials are items used in production or retail operations as part of a company's core business. Through various forms of web services, B2B operations can also be sustained in this area.

Electronic Marketplace

Information services, such as the electronic marketplace, permit companies to engage in B2B market operations in horizontal and vertical electronic marketplaces. In a *horizontal marketplace*, buyers and sellers can interact across many industries. Travel and financial services are common examples, because they are applicable to almost any type of business, such as the process industries (oil and gas) and conventional and electronic retailing.

In a *vertical marketplace*, buyers and sellers are in the same industry and primarily engage in information services that relate to direct material.

Electronic Government

Information services are a means of transforming the management and operations of government to be more responsive, efficient, and reliable in delivering services to the electorate – at all governmental levels, including federal, state, and local communities. The objective is to enhance informational facilities that already exist so they may properly be regarded as "click and mortar," with the options of obtaining information and services via the Internet and World Wide Web while continuing to have a physical presence. Three flavors have been identified: Government to Business (G2B), Government to Consumer (G2C), and Government to Government (G2G). In the latter case, there are two possibilities: inter-government and intra-government. Inter-government refers to the vertical alignment of information services between governmental levels on the same initiative, such as the coordination of federal, state, and local agencies on air pollution. Intra-government refers to the horizontal alignment of services between agencies at the same level of government, such as disaster response coordination between police, fire, and emergency medical departments.

Government to business operations reflect information services that cover purchasing of MRO materials, and the provisioning of information facilities for procedures, regulations, reporting, and compliance. In the latter case, governmental reporting facilities (by business to government) are commonly available to submit requisite documentation through Internet and World Wide Web services.

Most citizens are familiar with Government to consumer information services for taxes and various forms of registration. For taxpayers, the ability to download forms and directions, and the ability to submit completed tax forms is paramount. For those of us fortunate enough to receive a tax refund, the increased efficiency is money in the bank. Vehicle and voter registration are other information services that are efficient from both client and provider perspectives.

Overall, however, the availability of information on dates, procedures, directions, and so forth, at the click of a mouse via the Internet and the World Wide Web – pure information services – is the greatest advantage of G2C services.

PERSONAL INFORMATION SERVICES

Personal Information services are an ever expanding collection of Internet and World Wide Web applications. The prevalence of the applications, however, brings up a fundamental question about exactly what constitutes the clients, providers, and the services in the various forms of information service. The resources appear to be different among the applications, so the presentation of the subject matter will be instructive for determining the scope of personal information services. Accordingly, we will cover the following services: chat rooms, instant messaging, Internet telephone, web auctions, user-generated media, social networking, and newsgroups. This is only a sample of relevant applications but is indicative of how information services are used to support those applications.

Chat Rooms

One of the most popular means of communicating on the Internet is through a chat, room, the best known of which is IRC (Internet Relay Chat). IRC operates in the client/server mode and requires an IRC server; clients require special IRC software, usually downloaded from the Internet.

When using chat, the user selects a channel, which establishes the conversation in which the user will participate. Characteristically, other users, throughout the world, will have chosen the same channel. The idea being that they will exchange information on a certain subject.

During operation, a user types messages on his or her local client computer and the information is relayed via the Internet to the server. The message is then forwarded to other users signed on to the same channel and is displayed on their screens. A user may just listen, figuratively speaking, or may participate in the conversation. Ostensibly, users respond to other users' transmissions, so that an identifying name (sometimes called a *handle*) accompanies each submission. Since chat rooms are a global phenomenon, a network of IRC servers is required to service all of the users in a specific domain. A recent development is "voice chat," which is an audio equivalent to the traditional text-based chat.

At the end-user level, a chat room can be viewed as a collection of clients whose interpersonal communications are being managed

by the chat server system operating as a service provider. The chat server system consists of the hardware, software, and Internet facilities, necessary to do the task. The service process consists of a set of dynamically determined client/server interactions, where the end-user is the client and the chat server is the service provider.

Instant Messaging

Instant messaging is the private real-time communication of textual messages between two users logged on to an instant messaging (IM) server over the Internet. Messages are forwarded through an IM server that uses the "sender" client's buddy list to determine the destination for forwarded messages.

Many Internet specialists consider instant messaging to be a form of chat room operations, since it has similar information service characteristics.

Front and Back Stages

Internet chat and instant messaging, among other information services, incorporate a value chain of component services, divided between front and back stages. (Tabas, 2007) Essentially, the front stage is what the end-user conceptualizes and the back stage is what is going on under the covers, so to speak.

The noteworthy aspect of the division is that human clients are only part of the process, if they are involved at all, and the front stage represents the client's experience supplemented by the back

stage that represents the information service support structure based on ICT facilities. The participants (Human or ICT) may possess different but complementary views of the service process.

Internet Telephone

Using the Internet for making telephone calls is appealing to many people because of the cost, which may be free in some cases, over and above the cost of the Internet connection. Several methods and associated software facilities are available. They generally fall into two broad categories.

In the first case, you use special hardware and software to communicate through your personal computer (PC) using a microphone and speakers. If you are calling someone who is also using the same method, the call is totally free, as it is with web browsing and email, and it is also applicable to users anywhere in the world.

In the second case, you use your ordinary "land line" telephone handset, and the call is routed over the Internet using a service process generally known as Voice over IP (VoIP). IP is the protocol for routing messages through the various inter-connected networks as packets of information. IP stands for Internet Protocol. With VoIP, your voice is digitized and routed through the Internet as information packets, similar to other information services such as web pages and email. At the receiving end, the voice packets are converted to normal telephone signals.

With Internet telephone, the conceptualized front and back stages coincide. The clients are the telephone users and the service provider is the value chain of Internet activities.

Web Auctions

A *web auction* is an Internet and World Wide Web service that connects buyers and sellers in a consumer-to-consumer (C2C) mode to conduct an online version of traditional auction. A well-known web site that manages the web auction process is *eBay*, but there are notably other sites that perform the same service.

In this instance, the information service is the posting and delivery of information concerning products for sale and associated bids. The clients are the buyers and sellers and the information service consists of the information processing facilities to sustain the auction. In this instance, the Internet and the World Wide Web serve only as a communication channel.

User Generated Media

There are three major forms of information dissemination normally originating from individuals that use the Internet and World Wide Web services: web logs, podcasts, and RSS feeds. The services are related and are covered together in this section.

A *web log* (called a *blog*) is a medium for presenting information without restrictions or review over the Internet and accessible through the World Wide Web. People who participate

in the service of creating information content in this category are known as *bloggers*, and the process itself is known as *blogging*. The following three information services are normally associated with this form of activity: (1) Obtaining information on how to set up and access a blog web site; (2) Providing services that assist in actually setting up a blog web site; and (3) Using services that assist in making entries in a web log. Each blog site has a uniform resource locator (URL) and a theme, subsequently used for search and discovery. URL stands for uniform resource locator.

Clearly, the information services needed for accessing blogs are traditional web searches, wherein you request information, and it is returned to you using pull technology. Individuals use search engines, such as Google, to locate blog sites. There are search engines designed specifically for searching blog sites.

A *podcast* is an audio blog, serviced by the Internet that serves the same purpose as a personal radio station. Using your PC and a microphone, you can record a document and store it on an appropriate blog site. Other users can then download the audio blog to their PC for listening or for transfer to a music player. Podcasts are used to listen to broadcast media nd educational material. In the latter category, a podcast is an effective means of delivering course material to students.

An *RSS feed* is a means of generating a wider audience for blogs and podcasts, through an Internet technique known as Really Simple Syndication. RSS feeds utilize special web formatted

material and delivers automatically generated downloads to registered end users using push technology.

User-generated media operations are generally considered to be a front stage process. All communications are *asynchronous*, which means they are created (or uploaded) as a process at one time and accessed (or downloaded) by another process at another time, using push technology.

Social Networking

Social networking is usually regarded as the process of keeping up with friends and family, and it is no surprise that the process has migrated to the World Wide Web. The inherent information service in social networking is known as "shared space."

A *shared space* is an online virtual public space in which a person – usually a young person – can display information about themselves, including text, audio, and video. Special web sites, such as MySpace and Facebook, are designed to handle social networking. Actually, the video is predominantly photographs taken with a digital camera and uploaded to an appropriate web site set up for social networking.

A person's virtual space is subsequently accessible by friends. The conceptual model for a shared space is that of a private room to which one can invite friends to look around, thus giving the owner a private virtual space not otherwise available in everyday life.

As with information services that support media, social networking services are asynchronous and use pull technology.

Newsgroups

A *newsgroup* is a collection of people that participate in a discussion on a particular subject using Internet facilities. The usual form of communication is email, and the mode of communication is question and answer. The largest and most widely known online news group is known as *usenet*.

A participant subscribes to a particular topic. When that participant logs on to the newsgroup server, the entries on the selected topic are automatically sent to that participant.

Special client software is required to participate in a newsgroup. User interactions are organized by thread, so that a given user effectively engages in a conversation, as required, with participants in the same interest group. If a thread is *moderated*, questions are sent to a human moderator who screens the questions for appropriateness. Otherwise, questions are simply listed by topic. Most threads are archived by date.

Newsgroup software employs the same information service modality as email, and in fact, is dependent upon email for its operational infrastructure. Newsgroup facilities are also available through most information service portals, such as America Online and Google. With Google, you can access newsgroups via http:// groups.google.com.

SUMMARY

An *information service* is a resource capable of supporting a service event or instantiating in a service event based on information. In other words, an information service can assist in the execution of a service, such as in retailing, or it can actually be the service as when buying a pair of shoes on the Internet

Most of the information that is communicated between people is about something. With information services, the client requests information and the provider supplies it using some form of communications channel.

Software would appear to be a service, such as in document preparation and as suggested by the example of ordinary mail. Information is moved from one placed to another and perhaps it is transformed a bit in the process.

Information is the cornerstone of modern business, and government as well, and is the major ingredient in everyday commerce. Business information services are usually divided into two categories: operational services and management services. Operational services are employed to run the enterprise and management services are used to manage the enterprise.

When you make an airline reservation or check a flight schedule using the Internet, you are using a transaction processing system. Transaction processing systems are the cornerstone of modern business.

Teams are the accepted norm in the modern enterprise, and collaboration is the process by which they progress toward a common goal. With information services, collaboration between groups and individuals can be effected from geographically dispersed locations.

Major enterprise information service applications are electronic commerce, electronic business, and electronic government. Major personal information service applications are chat rooms, instant messaging, Internet telephone, web auctions, web logs, podcasts, RSS feeds, social networking, and newsgroups.

SELECTED READING

Gates, B. (2007), *The Age of Software-Powered Communications*, Electronic Mail Message, October 16, 2007 1:03:06 PM EDT.

Gralla, P., *How the Internet Works*, Indianapolis, IN: Que Publishing, 2004.

Hagel, J. and J.S. Brown (2007), *From Push to Pull: Emerging Models for Mobilizing Resources,* www.edgeperspectives.com.

Richardson, L. and S. Ruby, RESTful Web Services, Sebastopol, CA; O'Reilly Media, Inc., 2007.

Spohrer, J., Vargo, S.C., Caswell, N., and P.P. Maglio (2007), *The Service System is the Basic Abstraction of Service Science*, IBM Research, Almaden Research Center, San Jose, CA, www.almaden.ibm.com/asr.

Stair, R.M. and G.W. Reynolds, *Principles of Information Systems: A Managerial Approach*, Boston: Thomson Course Technology, 2008.

Tabas, L., *Designing for Service Systems*, UCB School Report 2007-008, February, 2007.

Tapscott, D. and A.D. Williams, *Wikinomics: How Mass Collaboration Changes Everything*, New York: Penguin Group, Ic., 2006.

Tidwell, J., *Designing Interfaces*, Sebastopol, CA: O'Reilly Media, Inc., 2006.

Vargo, S. and B. Lusch, "Evolving to a New Dominant Logic for Marketing," *Journal of Marketing*, 69 (January, 2004), 1-17.

Vargo, S. and B. Lusch, *Service-Dominant Logic Basics*, www.sdlogic.net, 2007.\\

PART III

Theory

Ontological Elements for Information Systems Architecture

———— ∽ ————

An information systems architecture is a specification of the information, computational elements, people, and underlying concepts in a services system. Accordingly, an associated data architecture is a specification of how data is stored, processed, and used in a system of record. A given data architecture effectively governs the flow of data in a system and establishes a relationship between an organization's processes and it's supporting information systems. Data architecture for an enterprise describes its applications, hardware, networks, business objects, business processes, and data. As such, it encompasses a complex set of definitions, methods, data types, and relationships. This paper introduces the concept of *ontology* applied to information systems and describes the essential elements of data architecture.

Ontology

In philosophy, ontology is the study of being (or existence), describes the basic categories, and defines the entities and classes of elements in its domain. In the area of information systems, it is a specification of conceptualization used to enable knowledge sharing and reuse. More specifically, an ontology can be viewed as a

data model that describes objects, classes, attributes, and relations. In his ground-breaking book on knowledge representation, John F. Sowa gives an appropriate definition for our purposes:

The subject of *ontology* is the study of the *categories* of things that exist or may exist in some domain. The product of such a study, called an *ontology*, is a catalog of the types of things that are assumed to exist in a domain of interest *D* from the perspective of a person who uses the language *L* for the purpose of talking about *D*. The types in the ontology represent the *predicates, word senses,* or *concept and relation types* of the language *L* when used to discuss topics in the domain *D*. (Sowa, 2000)

One common approach to the delineation of ontological elements is to divide the extant entities into groups called "categories." These lists of categories are quite different from another. It is in this latter sense that ontology is applied to such fields as theology, information science, and artificial intelligence. (Wikipedia 2007)

Ontological Engineering

Ontological engineering encompasses a set of activities conducted during conceptualization, design, implementation, and deployment of ontologies. [5] Ontological engineering seeks to achieve the following goals in a given domain:

- Definition of terms
- Establishment of a body of domain knowledge
- Specification of coherent and expressive knowledge bases

In short, an ontology defines the vocabulary of a problem domain and a set of constraints on how terms are related. It also gives data types and operations defined over the data types.

Data Architecture

Data architecture describes how data is processed, stored, and utilized in a given system. It provides criteria for data processing operations that make it possible to design data flows and also control the flow of data in the system. (Wikipedia, *op. cit.*) Stephens defines data architecture as a corporation's expression of strategy for creating and managing the use of data in order to transform data into information. He goes on to note that it is a strategic asset that must assure the following:

- Standardization of data structures
- Definition protection of the data resource
- Consistence and quality of the data resource
- Judicial use of corporate resources
- Delivery of timely and credible data
- It addresses business needs
- That it can be managed in a corporate environment

The fact that data architecture is a "grey architecture" does not detract from its validity.

Business Objects

A *business object* encapsulates the business logic of a single business entity and the data pertinent to that entity. [6] Each business object consists of one or more service components and one or more data components. A *service component* is the functionality supplied by a business object. A *data component* encapsulates data stored in a database.

Accordingly, data architecture is conceptualized as a set of business objects.

Frameworks

A *framework* is a taxonomy for looking at a class of computer applications. It effectively works by identifying the pieces that constitute an application and prescribing how they should be put together. Typically, a framework emphasizes segmentation and sharing at the data level. Operational and reference data are separated, so that reference data may be shared among frameworks. Rather than viewing an application as a monolithic structure supporting a particular business function, it is useful to view an application framework as a collection of one or more of the following elements: a computational engine, a data management component, application building blocks, and a user-interface module. This viewpoint recognizes and takes advantage of off-the-shelf components. The needed infrastructure includes a reference data architecture and a metadata repository. A *reference*

data architecture is a prescription of how data should flow within a single application framework and between diverse application frameworks. A *metadata repository* is the concept that allows middleware to transfer data between platforms on a scheduled or dynamic basis.

A framework can be conceptualized as a collection of three views: organization, business, and technical. The *business view* is significant and consists of data, function, workflow, and the solution structure. Within this view, the *data* refers to the operational and historical databases, the legacy files, the staging database, and the transfer files. The *function* denotes the applications and the programs that transfer data between applications. The *workflow* refers to the behavioral aspects of the combination of data and function. The *solution structure* is the data architecture that holds information about the combination of generic components from the data, function, and workflow areas.

Application Domains and Application Groups

An *application domain* (AD) is a suite of application programs, user interfaces, databases, reporting facilities, file, data marts, and related entities that collectively perform an enterprise function. An example would be "Order Management and Trading." In an application domain, all applications are related but some applications are more related than others. Related ADs communicate with each other through a *virtual data exchange* (VDE). The notion of a VDE stems from the need to avoid the

case where ADs communicate directly. A set of ADs connected by a VDE are called an *application group* (AG). An example of an AG would be "Investment Operations," perhaps consisting of the following ADs: Order Management and Trading, Holdings Management, Investment Accounting, Custody Processing, and Back Office Integration.

The primary benefit of this viewpoint is that an application group maintains its autonomy while participating in the overall enterprise design through the reference data architecture.

Data Architecture Ontology

The preceding sections give the context for the ontology of data architecture. This section gives definitions for the ontological elements, as listed in Table 1.

1. **Data view** is a collection of single elements, such as name, address, order number, etc. Data elements are commonly structured for storage and retrieval purposes and are normally associated with an application or a database, requiring an appropriate semantic context.

2. **Information view** is data to which knowledge has been applied. This view incorporates an appropriate semantic definition and represents a "business view" of data. Information is commonly aggregated for analysis, inference, understanding, and decision making.

3. **Data architecture** reflects the structure of storage components and the manner in which data is exchanged between them. Data architecture also defines how data will be managed, organized, stored, transformed, accessed, and otherwise made available to applications and users. Data architecture is composed of conceptual-level and logical-level descriptions and derives its applicability through a framework.

4. **Conceptual-level data architecture** defines design constructs, known as templates and best use principles concerning their use. It also describes standards, policies, and processes for use of subject data elements.

5. **Logical-level data architecture** applies the conceptual constructs and processes to an application domain, and establishes and incorporates data management structures and technology.

6. A **Framework** is a collection of components, connections, actors, and use cases that comprise a reusable design of a data architecture for a class of business problems. A framework works with a subject data model to establish a context for a data architecture.

7. **Information architecture** represents the business-process view of a data architecture, and delineates the information needed to support different business processes. A framework is used to relate technology to users, information structures, and use cases.

8. **Enterprise data architecture** is a conceptual-level data architecture that is reusable across the enterprise. This element facilitates data sharing business units and enables risk avoidance and cost reduction.

9. **Subject data model** is a high-level view of data with a business perspective, and represents an aggregate view of information from multiple application systems. This data model supports a CRUD matrix integration of application and infrastructure.

10. **Operational database** is an online system that usually supports transaction processing and supports operational queries and update capability by being "current" data valued and subject oriented.

11. **Data warehouse** is a historical database that is organized for efficient updating from source systems. It may incorporate aggregation and summarization to support upstream data marts. A data warehouse may also allow access/reporting but is not usually optimized for that.

12. **Data mart** is a historical database optimized for access and reporting around a business unit. It is usually updated from a data warehouse via "batch updates."

13. **Metadata** is a common repository of "data about data" that is sharable between applications and platforms, reflecting business semantics and data sharing.

14. **Staging database** is a focal point for data cleansing operations on dynamic data from operational databases.

15. **Data exchange** is an event driven platform for exchanging data between applications.

16. **Data hub** is a middleware system designed to move data between source and target systems. The source and target systems include operational databases, legacy files, and data warehouse/mart data stores.

17. **Reference data architecture** refers to goal-state architecture, enterprise data warehouse, department data mart, and reporting systems.

Collectively, the definitions provide a means of communicating in the problem domain of data architecture.

TABLE 1. Ontological Elements

Number	Element
1	Data View
2	Information View
3	Data Architecture
4	Conceptual-Level Data Architecture
5	Logical-Level Data Architecture
6	Framework
7	Information Architecture
8	Enterprise Data Architecture
9	Subject Data Model
10	Operational Database
11	Data Warehouse

12	Data Mart
13	Metadata
14	Staging Database
15	Data Exchange
16	Data Hub
17	Reference Data Architecture

Ongoing Development

Future developments include a functional description of each of the ontological elements.

References

[1] http://en.wikipedia.org/wiki/Data_Architecture

[2] Johnson, A. and R. Wiggins, "Modeling the enterprise data architecture," IBM Corporation web site

[3] http://en.wikipedia.org/wiki/Ontology

[4] Gruber, T., gruber@ksl.stanford.edu, "What is an ontology?"

[5] Dedvedzic, V.) April 2002), "Understanding Ontological Engineering," *Communications of the ACM* 45:4, pp. 136-144.

[6] Lewis, G., et al. (2001, *An Enterprise Information System Data Architecture Guide,* CMU Technical Report ESC-TR-2001-018.

[7] Katzan, H. (December 200), "Advanced Financial Management: Is there a framework in our future?" *INC Magazine.*

[8] Sowa, John F. (2000), *Knowledge Representation: Logical, Philosophical and Computational Foundations,* Brooks Cole Publishing, Pacific Grove Publishing, Inc.

CHAPTER 12

Principles of Service Systems Ontology

———···———

The basic concepts of service, service systems, and service science have been well-developed. (Sampson and Froehle 2006, Maglio and Zysman 2007, and Katzan 2008b) To fully benefit from the service perspective, however, an ontological foundation is required to facilitate communication among researchers and assist with the ongoing theoretical and pragmatic development of the discipline. To some extent, an ontology is dependant upon a particular point of view, and this paper seeks to identify a set of rigid descriptors that link to the various underlying concepts. We are going to take the view that a comprehensive depiction of the application domain is as important in service ontology as is the taxonomy used to describe it.

Service

In a widely distributed paper on the science of service, Spohrer and associates (Spohrer 2007b) give several characteristics of an elementary service event: customer participation, simultaneity, perishability, intangibility, and heterogeneity. *Customer participation* refers to the co-production of the service experience and the co-creation of service value. *Simultaneity* denotes the fact that a service is produced and consumed simultaneously. *Perishability* refers to time perishable capacity from the provider's

155

viewpoint and opportunity loss from the client's perspective. *Intangibility* normally denotes the obvious fact that goods are not produced by a service event. Lastly, *heterogeneity* refers to the variation in a service from client to client and from provider to provider, along with the recognition that a service system is a complex system that can be mediated by information technology. This seemingly simple definition belies the complexity of the situation, since there is a multiplicity of service definitions, based on existential considerations. A service is a socially constructed temporal event, and within that domain, an objectivist view of the subject matter is adopted. Service exists and possesses an implicit lifecycle comprised of design, development, analysis, and implementation, similar in nature to most technical innovations. Specificity will be added to the service lifecycle model in a later section. Moreover, a service evolves and is subject to descriptive and nominative modalities. As with traditional social activities, a service can be analyzed and measured. In fact, a service is an economic entity that possesses demonstrable value to the participants, in particular, and to organizations and society, as a whole.

Services are indigenous to the existence of modern society. In fact, if one replaces the concept of labor with that of service, the principles of service science can be derived from the essential work of Adam Smith (Smith 1776), most pointedly in his notions of "value in use" and "value in exchange."

Social Constructivism

Social constructivism is a theory of knowledge (epistemology) based, at least in part, on the social and material setting in which a belief is produced or maintained. In social constructivism, individuals and groups participate in a perceived reality, and create an element of knowledge, as espoused by the philosophical doctrine of Equal Validity. (Boghossian 2006, Bergquist 1993) Equal validity suggests the notion that other means of knowing exist in addition to the factual predominance of scientific investigation. Consider an example of a simple wooden chair developed in antiquity and regarded as a place to sit and pile books. A chair is made from a type of wood that we as a society have discovered as being useful to the purpose. Wood exists as a natural phenomenon independently of chairs and the social setting in which it exists. The precise form and substance of a chair, however, is a socially constructed form of knowledge that none but the hardened skeptic would deny is a valid form of knowledge. Service systems are socially constructed forms of interaction wherein entities exchange beneficial forms of action through the combination of people and technologies that adapt to the changing level of information in the system. As such, reality constructed through social mechanisms is a dynamic process replicated and maintained by social interactions within a service and between services.

Service systems are actual social phenomena that existed, in part, before the development of service science and are analogous to economic systems that existed before the development and study of economics. Both types of systems are governed by events in their operational environments and are continually being created, modified, and retired. A service is neither synthetic (like synthetic rubber or various chemical compounds) nor artificial (like artificial intelligence in the computer field). Services are observable, and through a process of shared reality, concepts are developed that lead to classes of service and subsequently instances of that service. We are going to apply epistemological concepts to develop a service ontology that adheres to the hypothetico-deductive modality of scientific research. (Sutherland 1975)

Service Universe

A *service universe* is a collection of services under consideration at a given point in time by a person, group, organization, or even a society. A service universe is typically a set of services, organized in some fashion to achieve a discernable purpose. However, that need not necessarily be the case, and could be a disparate collection of temporal service events, or even a combination of the two categories. The notion of a service is problematical, because there are differing points of view on exactly what constitutes a service, even though most persons could reliably identify a service when confronted with one. Professional, technical, and scientific people are service providers, even though they do not normally think of themselves in that fashion. Call centers, consulting

companies, and utilities also do service, but dry cleaners and fast-food restaurants do them, as well. The subject is important because 80-90% of the working population in developed countries is engaged in services, and they are also consumers of services.

A simple question on this subject, such as "What is a service?" can yield a surprisingly large number of different answers. Here are a few instances that would immediately come to mind:

1. An action performed by one person or group on behalf of another person, organization, or group.
2. A generic type of action, such as a medical service or a web service.
3. The process of performing some action classified as a service.
4. The result of an action – typically a change affecting an object or person.
5. The utility of a change affecting a person or object – the value proposition.
6. An organization behaving in a prescribed way to benefit or operate in the best interests of a person or group.
7. A promise, contractual agreement, or obligation to perform a specified action in the future as a response to a triggering event.
8. The deployment of service assets for the benefit of service participants, commonly regarded as provider and client.

There are two fundamentally different points of view: the global view and the local view. The *global view* refers to the notion of a system comprised of interacting and complementary services. One could consider the global view as an external service description, useful for determining how a collection of services functions in order to benefit various people, organizations, and business processes. This view is analogous to macroeconomics. The *local view* describes and delineates the steps in a distinct service process, emphasizing the service participants and the complementary roles they play in the service event. This view is analogous to microeconomics. A discrete service fits nicely into one of several mutually exclusive categories based on service characteristics that can be distinguished with a service DNA. (Katzan 2008a) In this paper, we are going to adopt global and local viewpoints and structure the ontology according to that dichotomy. Between the global and local points-of-view, we are going to develop a consistent set of underlying concepts, relationships, and language elements.

Service Systems

A singular service event is a form of social organization in which two or more resources interact to achieve an agreed-upon purpose, where a resource can be a person, organization, or an element of technology. The service is the unit of exchange in the interaction that is established to produce value for each of the participants. (Spohrer 2007b) The resources are commonly

referred to as service entities or entities. Based on this assessment, we can propose the following definition:

Definition of Service Two entities collaborate and what is produced from the interaction is a service, *if and only if*

- Both parties participate in the exchange
- Both parties benefit from the exchange such that value is co-created in a complementary form
- The action of the service is complementary
- The parties assume complementary but differing roles
- The roles are commonly known as *provider* and *client*.

The provider role is regarded as a serving activity, and the client role is, likewise, regarded as a receiving activity. Moreover, the collaboration adapts to the win-win model of economic exchange, since value is co-created for both participants. The complementary form of activity is intended to distinguish it from a supplementary form in which participants operate as partners to perform a stated function. For example, a physician and a patient exhibit complementary roles in a service, whereas a scenario in which two masons work together to build a structure represents a supplementary form of behavior. A singular service event is the most elementary form of a service system. (Spohrer 2007)

A unified service is a process that takes input and produces output. In between the input and the output, there exists one or more steps that constitute the service process. (Sampson and

Froehle 2006, Katzan 2008b) The steps in a service process often include other services leading to the concept of a service system.

A *service system* is a collection of resources, economic entities, and other services capable of engaging in and supporting one or more service events. Services, i.e., service processes, may interact or they may be included in a service value chain. This is a recursive definition of a service system that would support the following modalities of service operation: *tell me, show me, help me, and do it for me.* Service systems are inherently multidisciplinary, since a service provider may not have the knowledge, skill, time, resources, and inclination to perform all of the steps in a service process and require the services of an external service provider.

As introduced above, service systems are social constructs that commonly encompass other services and are components of a larger reality. An organizational structure of this particular genre could be regarded from either of two points of view: as an economy or as an adaptive social structure. As an *economy*, it is a system of relationships that govern the availability of scarce resources and operate under conditions of efficiency and effectiveness. As an *adaptive social structure,* the efficacy of a service event depends upon the dynamic environment in which an organization operates. (Selznick 1948) A service system is a cooperative dynamically changing formal system, with a porous boundary so that the environment it which it resides has a deterministic effect on its behavior.

A unified service system requires some sort of organizational entanglement so that an enterprise can invest prudently and produce predictable outcomes. Accordingly, research into the mechanics of service systems requires three things: an appropriate operational platform, a design theoretic formulation, and an ontology of service and service systems, which is introduced in subsequent sections.

Service Science

With regard to academic disciplines, there is an old saying that goes somewhat as follows: "If it has the word 'science' in its title, then it isn't science." It would appear that service science is an exception. There are two fundamental questions: "What is science, anyway?" and "What does a conceptualization of science have to do with service?"

In an earlier debate concerning computer science, Newell, Perlis, and Simon (Newell 1967) state, "Wherever there are phenomena, there can be a science to describe and explain those phenomena." Further, Kuhn (Kuhn 1962) states, "Science is the agreed upon methods and standards of rigor used by a community to develop a body of knowledge that accounts for observable phenomenon with conceptual frameworks, theories, models, and laws that can be empirically tested and applied within a world view or paradigm." Moreover, since service systems are an observable and evolving phenomena, subject to the dynamics of the economic world, the development of a science of service,

replete with its own frameworks, models, and theories, is an essential element in a total world view. (Spohrer 2007a)

Epistemologically, there exists a conceptual service universe in which observable services and service systems operate. One can view this service universe in a manner similar to which we view the physical universe described by physics and chemistry. The modus operandi in those disciplines is to abstract a piece of that universe and study it as a sub-discipline. Mechanics, heat, and sound are elementary sub-disciplines that fall into the discipline of physics.

The services in the service universe can be viewed metaphorically as entities floating around in a service space waiting for the chance to be called upon to execute as a singular event, as a component of a service system, or as a chance to be called upon interactively. Some services are used in more than one service system. *Service science* is a collection of models of sub-disciplines abstracted from the service universe, in much the same manner that the physical sciences are collections of sub-disciplines. The procedure in all cases is to take a piece of an existing system and put it under the microscope of academic scrutiny. Thus, a particular service or a service system is an abstraction of service science, as with the physical universe, and a service theory is a means of tying the various models together. On the other hand, if one views the entire amorphous service space as a service system, then service science could be alternately viewed as a basic abstraction of service systems, realizing, of course, that the ultimate objective is to study categories of service systems.

There are, of course, additional considerations regarding the phenomena of service and service systems. Services evolve and are continually being developed and modified. Service systems are affected through their porous boundaries by stakeholders, laws, and social customs. They also require formalization as important aspects of the discipline of service science.

ONTOLOGY

Ontology is a specification of "what is." In philosophy, use of the term reflects the study of being (or existence) and describes and delineates a collection of basic categories, and defines the entities and classes of elements within a category. In service science, ontology is a specification of a conceptualization used to enable knowledge sharing. Since ontology concerns existence, an ontological definition of a subject – perhaps a service category – reflects a materialization of a concept obtained through a shared reality, and not what it is called or how it is made or used. In this paper, the definition of ontology, as "a set of representational primitives with which to model a domain of knowledge or discourse," will be adopted. (Gruber 2008, Wikipedia 2009a) More specifically, ontology can be viewed as a data model that describes objects, classes, attributes, and relations. In his ground-breaking book on knowledge representation, John F. Sowa gives an appropriate definition for our purposes:

The subject of *ontology* is the study of the *categories* of things that exist or may exist in some domain. The product of such a study, called *ontology*, is a catalog of the types of things that are

assumed to exist in a domain of interest D from the perspective of a person who uses the language L for the purpose of talking about D. The types in the ontology represent the *predicates, word senses,* or *concept and relation types* of the language L when used to discuss topics in the domain D. (Sowa 2000)

One common approach to the delineation of ontological elements is to divide the extant entities into groups called "categories." These lists of categories can be quite different from one another. It is in this latter sense that ontology is applied to such fields as theology, service science, and artificial intelligence. (Wikipedia 2009)

Ontological Naming

In the naming of ontological elements, it is important to note that there are two approaches to the use of nouns. In one philosophical school, nouns should refer to existent entities. In the alternate school, nouns are used as a shorthand as reference to a collection of object or events. For example the word *mind* would refer to a collection of mental states, and society would refer to a collection of people.

Ontological Engineering

Ontological engineering encompasses a set of activities conducted during conceptualization, design, implementation, and deployment of ontologies. (Dedvedzic 2002) Ontological engineering seeks to achieve the following goals in a given domain:

Definition of terms

Establishment of a body of domain knowledge

Specification of coherent and expressive knowledge bases

In short, ontology defines the vocabulary of a problem domain and a set of constraints on how terms are related. It also gives data types and operations defined over the data types.

Most forms of ontology are expressed in an ontology language and share structural similarities, such as individuals, classes, attributes, relations, function, restrictions, rules, axioms, and events. The basic idea behind ontology languages is to allow software agents to communicate in a knowledge intensive computer-based environment: We are going to concentrate on the following components: (Guarino 1995, Wikipedia 2009)

Individuals referring to instances and objects

Classes expressed as sets, collections, and kinds of things

Attributes giving features and characteristics of individuals and classes

Relations that determine ways that individuals and classes relate

The components determine whether a specific ontology is a domain ontology or an upper ontology. In a *domain ontology*, a specific type would be relevant to particular category, such as in a medical or household category. In an *upper ontology*, a type would be applicable to all ontologies in the universe of discourse. In the service ontology, presented in the following section, we are going to be developing an upper ontology for service systems.

UPPER ONTOLOGY FOR SERVICE SYSTEMS

The ontology of service systems is a developmental artifact for the study, design, analysis, and application of services. Essentially, a framework is needed to tie the elements together, so that they are applicable to a wide range of operational scenarios. (Alter 2008) The primary measure of an ontological determination is how it assists in delineating the value chain for services, comprised of people, technology, and organizations, and its relevance to education, government, business, and other social phenomena.

Service Systems Lifecycle

Service science is one of the few disciplines in which the basic principles and resultant theory apply to both small-scale and large-scale operations. We are going to proceed with that assumption. In its most basic form, a service is a value producing interaction between a service provider and a service client, consisting of a process conceptualized as a layered set of activities. (Ferrario and Guardino 2008) It is useful to conceptualize the layers according to the following global service system lifecycle:

Service commitment
Service production
Service availability
Service delivery
Service analysis
Service termination

Initially, we are going to be looking at services from a global view, where the lifecycle pertains to a set of generic services supplied by an economic entity, such as a governing body, a business, an institution, or an individual acting in a service capacity. *Service commitment* refers to the formal agreement to provide a class of services to a service audience by a principal or trustee with the proper administrative control over the service environment. The agreement to provide fire service by a municipality and the founding of a health clinic are common examples. *Service production* pertains to service provisioning, infrastructure, availability, quality management, and back-office processing. The producer is the agent of the principal in a prototypical principal-agent scenario. The principal and agent may be the same economic entity or different economic entities depending upon the scope of the service domain. The manager of a chain of restaurants and the medical director of a clinic are examples. *Service availability* is the time during which a service is available. Commitment does not necessarily imply availability, because of a variety of spatiotemporal events. *Service delivery* is the class of actions usually regarded as the service and is the layer where the service client comes into the picture. The doctor/patient relationship is a good example of this layer. The service provider, who could have a dual role as producer, is an agent of the producer as the primary source of service revenue and the primary provider of a service. *Service analysis* refers to measurement activities and the determination of value propositions needed to sustain service operations. *Service termination* reflects the inevitable consequence of a dynamic and evolving economic environment where a total

service operation has to be retired, because of insufficient activity or realigned opportunities. The global lifecycle represents a provisioning perspective of service systems.

Service Entities

We are looking at five service entities: the *service principal*, functioning as a trustee of a service or a service system; the *service producer*, responsible for the availability, infrastructure, service provisioning, and back-office processing; the *service provider*, charged with the application of resources for the benefit of another service entity: the *service client*, who has a complementary service relationship with the service provider; and the *service object* that may be the direct recipient of the result of the service process.

A *service entity* need not be a person, but can be a group, organization, business, governing body, educational institution, or a physical object, such as a possession or an element of computer software.

Service Commitment

Service commitment is a guarantee by a principal to provide a set of actions that constitutes a service. A common example might be the promise of a mayor of a town to provide fire service to his constituents. (Ferrario and Guardino 2008) The principal can be an organization, such as a government, a medical group, an educational institution, a private service business, a consulting firm with a service-level agreement, and an ad hoc entity that

provides service to other service entities. A service commitment may result from an explicit declaration, such as "I agree to provide said service to a receiving agent" or be implicit in a legal charter or understanding, such as a medical practice or financial institution. A service commitment may apply to all constituents in the principal's domain – perhaps to all families moving into a community or entering a service facility.

The committed service may not, and probably will not, be performed by the principal, who may rely on a service producer and an ensuing service provider known as a *service agent* to actually execute the service process. Thus, a service agent provides a service to the principal and to the service object. The service principal, producer, and provider may coincide or be distinct to some degree.

Service Production

Service production supports a service commitment by establishing service parameters, such as time, location, availability, infrastructure, provisioning, record keeping, and legal compliance and certification. Time and location are key factors in service delivery that are summarized through a service DNA, which partitions the service domain into mutually exclusive service categories. (Katzan 2008a) The principle element in service production is maintenance of the service infrastructure, consisting of physical facilities, operational procedures, satisfaction of legal requirements, competent provider provisioning, and dependable auxiliary service provisioning.

Service Availability

The *availability* of a service is dependent upon the inherent nature of the service commitment. The access to and duration of medical provisioning, banking, insurance, product warranties, and household service, as examples, probably differ in most cases. It is important to additionally note the significance of service commitment with regard to service availability. What a service principal commits to is the *service content* and not to its associated service process, scheduling, and other operational considerations.

Service Delivery

In order for a service provider and a client to co-create a service event, there must be some degree of locality to the situation, in the sense that the client travels to the provider, the provider travels to the client, the client and provider execute the service event in a third-party location, or they communicate via some form of interactive device and its corresponding media. Location is basic to service provisioning. When the client travels to the provider site, the location is termed a *service factory* and the client or the service object remain in the service factory for the duration of the service transaction. When the service object is left in the provider's facilities, the location is known as a *service shop*. The provider may travel to *client facilities*, as in the cases of custodial work or nursing home care. With information service, the provider may reside in a remote facility and provide access through a service portal.

A related consideration is the distinction between *discrete service* and *continuous service*. There are many edge cases. Insurance is commonly regarded as a continuous service, as is banking – except in the cases where the customer visits a bank branch. Medical provisioning, automobile maintenance, and household service are usually regarded as discrete services. In the latter case, when a service event is over, it's over. A follow-on service is regarded as another service event.

Service Analysis

To some extent, all services consist of the application of resources, and the success of those services is dependent upon how efficiently and effectively those resources are applied in a normative manner to a specific problem domain. (Spohrer 2007a) Thus, measurement and analysis is required to assess both individual service interactions and the cumulative result of a set of service interactions. The basic tenet of service delivery is the following. *The client starts out with expectations, and a service deliverer should start out off by assessing what those expectations are.* However, not all service events are successful, so that a risk analysis should be performed by the providers and the client prior to a service engagement. In service analysis, the success of a service event is dependent upon how accurately the service providers and the client assess their roles.

Measurement and analysis are often the modus for judging service and service quality, and in an organizational setting, is achieved through service level agreements between complementary

economic entities. For instances where implicit agreements persist, service analysis involves responsiveness, timeliness, and completeness – traditional metrics that have evolved through informal agreement.

Service Termination

In order for a service system to be successful, it must *exist* and *persist*. To exist, that service must satisfy the economic goals of provider, client, producer, and trustee in due consideration of the needs surrounding its competitors, partners (business or operational), employees, and investors. (Spohrer 2007a) The economic goals are known as the *value proposition* of the service consisting of the provider's sacrifice, the client's sacrifice, provider's exploitation, and the client's exploitation, from both short-term and long-term perspectives. (Alter 2008) Accordingly, a discrete service offering can be unsuccessful in either of four ways: (Spohrer op cit.)

The client does not accept the provider's value proposition in light of its own.
The client decides to engage in "self service'
The client decides to accept service from an alternate source
The client decides to forgo service

Thus, cumulative service decisions from within the *client domain* essentially determine the persistence of a service commitment.

DOMAIN ONTOLOGY FOR SERVICE

A discrete service event entails the commitment of resources for the benefit of a client. Each service event – frequently referred to as a service interaction – consists of a series of steps called *the service process* intended to achieve a particular goal. Within a given service category, the various service processes are similar within acceptable limits of variability.

Basic Service Categories

A *service* is a provider/client relationship (Katzan 2008b) that captures value for both participants that can be individuals, organizations, software, or a complex arrangement of the three, given as follows:

<service-participant> ::= <individual> | <organization>
|<software-as-a-service>|
<service-participant> + <individual> |
<service-participant> + organization>

Service operations are customarily grouped into three classes: people processing, possession processing, and information processing. Within each domain, it is therefore important to view the client/provider relationship along the following dimensions:

Tangible vs. intangible
Primary vs. secondary
Facilitating vs. auxiliary

This approach focuses on the fact that a service event is a process consisting of primary and secondary services. (Sampson and Froehle 2006)

TANGIBLE AND INTANGIBLE SERVICE A *tangible service* is a provider/client event that results in demonstrable values to the service participants. With an individual service participant, this is a left-brain function (LBF). In retailing, it is the acquisition of a product including attendant activities that change the ownership attribute of the associated product. However, the value proposition for a product may be determined from the service it provides, rather than from the intrinsic value of its specific components. In pure service, such as a people and possession processing service, value is created through the work performed on behalf of the client by the provider. With information service, the service's value is derived from the transfer of information from service provider to the client. An *intangible service* provides value for a service participant through the perspective of a right-brain function (RBF). Certain products, such as premium automobiles (Rosengarten 2006), special jewelry, and elegant real estate, for example, are typically associated with a high-level of intangible service. As mentioned previously, the intangible value of a product may exceed its tangible value.

PRIMARY AND SECONDARY SERVICE A *primary service* is the core service for which the provider and the client interact to produce demonstrable value. Simple examples are a dental appointment or a lawn care service. A *secondary service* is a service that does not exist separately as a primary service and plays a supportive

role to a primary service. Common examples are the weigh in and blood pressure checks associated with a doctor's visit and the acceptance and delivery of garments at a dry cleaning establishment. Secondary service can also exist as a supplementary or referral service.

FACILITATING AND AUXILIARY SERVICE A *facilitating service* is disjoint from a primary or secondary service and enables a client to obtain utility from a tangible service. Usability service, commonly associated with automobiles and computers, is a common example of a facilitating service. Another common example of a facilitating service is the purchase of an event ticket. In this instance, the event – be it a visit to the theatre, sporting match, or an amusement park – is the tangible service and the ticket is the intangible service.

An *auxiliary service* is independent from a core service and may be experienced before or after the primary service. A blood test taken prior to a doctor's appointment and a medical referral are examples of auxiliary services.

SERVICE FUNCTIONS Many service functions relate to satisfaction models for consumer judgments regarding service interactions. One of two possible viewpoints is selected: expectation confirmation or rational utility assessment. With the expectation confirmation approach, the psychological distance between expectation and realization is measured. The tangible aspects of service are emphasized. With the rational utility approach, the tangible factors of service delivery, as well as the intangible factors, are taken into consideration. *Tangible assessment* is a means of referring

to the demonstrable attributes of service delivery, such as product characteristics, skills of the service provider, and explicit service results as they pertain to people, possession, and information processing service. Tangible service results are utilitarian and measurable. *Intangible assessment* is a means of referring to the feeling that one experiences from a service interaction or the ownership of a product. Intangible service results are affective and hedonistic. The level of intangible service is normally a function of the feelings that one derives from ownership of a premium product or the participation in a service event with a particular service provider. The service functions are summarized in the DNA of a category of service, presented in the appendix and covered below.

Service Process Lifecycle

It is necessary to identify the key events in the operational service lifecycle and the major entities involved. The *service lifecycle* can be viewed as those activities that exist between service acquisition and service termination – from both structural and operational viewpoints. From the *structural* point-of-view, the set of layered activities incorporate the service commitment, service infrastructure, service availability, service delivery, and the eventual termination of a service, as delineated previously for the upper service ontology. From an *operational* point-of-view, the layered activities describe service events and incorporate those transactable actions that constitute the essence of service.

Based on the above definitions, the lifecycle of a service process consists of a loosely defined set of steps intended to co-create value for complementary service participants. It is useful to conceptualize a generic lifecycle for a domain ontology as consisting of the following steps:

> Service acquisition
> Service invocation
> Service execution
> Service termination

Service acquisition refers to the process of identifying a service provider with the requisite infrastructure, and its corollary, the process of attracting clients. *Service invocation* involves the scheduling and logistics part of the service process. *Service execution* entails the actual steps in the service process including supplementary services. *Service termination* incorporates referral, warranty, and archiving activities. The requisite infrastructure for sustaining the service process lifecycle is referred to as the *service platform* and is related to the activities of the producer in the upper ontology, covered previously. The service process lifecycle can be viewed as a set of layered events. We are going to supplement the service process lifecycle with service analytics that are descriptive of the end state of a service event.

Service Acquisition

The generic steps that comprise service acquisition represent the handshaking needed to establish a service relationship. From

the client perspective, acquisition consists of an awareness that some form of service is needed, known as *service awareness*, followed by the discovery of a suitable delivery vehicle, called *service discovery*, perhaps using Web Services, and finally the development of a service level agreement, usually known as *service negotiation*. From the provider perspective, service acquisition is fueled by a service commitment, service availability, and a variety of service conditions incorporated in the DNA of that service category. Prototypical examples of service acquisition are finding a doctor in a new town or locating a shop for automobile repair.

In a discrete service, the service provider assumes the role of the "service producer" and the service client assumes the role of the "service requestor," in the sense that the client takes the initiative in the acquisition process. In professional and technical services, the service provider often assumes the role of the requestor by directly approaching from a business perspective or through direct advertising.

Service Invocation

An exogenous condition is needed to initiate a service process by the service provider on behalf of a service client. (Ferrario 2008) It is termed a *triggering event* that can take one of a variety of forms, such as:

- An independent event requiring attention, such as a medical situation or a fire

- A request by the client, or its representative, to have a service performed that the client doesn't want to do, can't do, or the provider can do more efficiently
- A required service, perhaps by law or convention, initiated by the client or a governing body

The triggering event is typically followed by a *service scheduling* process that establishes a spatiotemporal location for service delivery. Some service providers use appointments to manage demand as a means of achieving service efficiency. The steps that facilitate core or primary service invocation are customarily regarded as a secondary service.

Service invocation involves back-office administrative record keeping and coordination, such that the provider and client can interact on a planned basis. The service delivery, availability, and demand dimensions of the service DNA sequence reflect the dynamics between provider and client in a service event. Appointments with professional service providers are formally scheduled, whereas arrangements with nonprofessionals are commonly scheduled on an informal basis.

Service Execution

Service execution is the phase of the service process lifecycle where the service provider engages the service client to achieve a goal state that reflects both provider and client perspectives. Alternately, the service object may be a service entity over which the client has legal or social responsibility. In general, the service

object can be a person, a possession, information, or an abstract entity such as a financial investment. We are going to refer to the provider, the client, and the service object as *service participants*.

The primary objective of a service event is referred to as the *core service* that has tangible value to the service participants. The core service is conventionally comprised of primary, secondary, and auxiliary services, as described earlier under Basic Service Categories. We are going to establish five categories with which the execution of a service event, per se, can be determined:

Category	*Alternative*
Modality	discrete, continuous
Diversity	heterogeneous, homogeneous
Temporality	active, passive
Complexity	low complexity, high complexity
Duration	short, long

Modality denotes whether the texture of the service takes place as a single interaction (*discrete*), such as a doctor's visit that is over when it is over, or it takes place over an extended period of time (*continuous*), such as an insurance policy. *Diversity* refers to whether the service can be performed by a specific provider (*heterogeneous*), such as particular attorney or accountant, or any one of a group of providers (*homogeneous*), such as a bank teller. *Temporality* specifies whether the service is one in which the provider and client actively participate (*active*), such as a dentist's visit, or one in which the service participants are not actively

engaged (*passive*) until a triggering event occurs, such as an insurance policy or a municipality's fire service. *Complexity* refers to whether the service is completed in a few similar steps (*low complexity*), or many different steps (*high complexity*). A hospital procedure or a home remodeling would reflect a high complexity; an appointment at the eye doctor's or a car detailing would exhibit low complexity. *Duration*, not to be confused with modality, refers to whether the service execution takes place in a few hours or less (*short duration*), or whether it takes place over a few days or longer (*high duration*). In medicine, a doctor's visit would have short duration, and a hospital stay would have long duration. In transportation, a ferry ride would have short duration, and a trans-Atlantic cruise would have long duration. Clearly, the collection of categories is generic and reflects the underlying difficulty in attempting to be specific with a ubiquitous social phenomena, such as service.

It is important to state the difference between DNA dimensions (see the *Appendix*) and categories of service execution. DNA dimensions are intended to describe and delineate the total service environment from the standpoint of upper and domain ontology. The categories of service execution are simply intended to provide specificity to the service process.

Service Termination and Analytics

Service termination and analytics encompasses follow-on activity, record keeping, archiving, and the financial aspects of service. Accordingly, this essential lifecycle element involves both

front-office and back-office activities on the part of the provider and the client, leading to quality and value assessments.

The service value analysis involves four components: provider's costs, provider's revenue, client's cost, client's revenue – recognizing that cost and revenue are not necessarily monetary. The *fundamental theorem of service delivery* applies to service analytics such that the cost of service by the provider must equal the value of commensurate service to the client, represented as:

$$C_P = V_C$$

where C_P is the cost to the provider and V_C is the value to the client. Accordingly,

$$C_P = C_p + C_s + C_t$$

where C_p is the cost of primary core service, C_s is the cost of secondary service, and C_t are the transaction costs.

Similarly,

$$V_C = V_t + V_i$$

where V_t is the value of tangible service and V_i is the value of intangible service.

Analytics help the provider and the client answer fundamental questions, such as: Should we? (*business value*), Can we? (*technology*), May we? (*governance*), and Will we? (*business priority*).

TAXONOMY OF SERVICE SYSTEMS

This section delineates a taxonomy of service systems. A taxonomy essentially provides a prose glossary of a body of knowledge and a methodology for systems analysis and design. In this particular instance, the taxonomy of service systems supplies a lens into a collection of concepts, definitions, and relations that describe the complex subject of service science.

1. Service Identification
 1.1 Service name
 1.2 Sponsoring organization
 1.3 Service initiation date
2. Service Participants
 2.1 Service principal
 2.2 Service producer
 2.3 Service provider
 2.4 Service client
 2.5 Service object
3. Service System Lifecycle
 3.1 Service commitment
 3.2 Service production
 3.3 Service availability
 3.4 Service delivery
 3.5 Service analysis
 3.6 Service termination

4. Service Process

 4.1 Service acquisition

 4.1.1 Service awareness

 4.1.2 Service discovery

 4.1.3 Service negotiation

 4.2 Service invocation

 4.2.1 Triggering event

 4.2.2 Service scheduling

 4.3 Service execution

 4.3.1 Service participants

 4.3.2 Service categories

 4.3.2.1 Service modality

 4.3.2.2 Service diversity

 4.3.2.3 Service temporality

 4.3.2.4 Service complexity

 4.3.2.5 Service duration

 4.3.2.6 Service DNA

 4.4 Service termination

 4.4.1 Provider costs

 4.4.1.1 Core service

 4.4.1.2 Secondary service

 4.4.1.3 Auxiliary service

 4.4.1.4 Transaction costs

 4.4.2 Client value

 4.4.2.1 Tangible value

 4.4.2.2 Intangible value

In using the taxonomy of service systems, a service analyst would necessarily supply entries for each of the ontological elements, as required by a particular service system under investigation.

SUMMARY

An ontological introduction to the principles of service systems has been presented with an emphasis on concepts, classes, objects, relations, and terminology. The paper introduces social constructivism, as a basis of service science, and continues with service concepts, service systems, ontology, and then on to upper ontology for services, domain ontology for service, and finally a taxonomy of service systems, as well as a short treatise on a DNA of service.

REFERENCES

Alter. S. 2008. Service system fundamentals: Work system, value chain, and life cycle. *IBM System Journal*, 47(1): 71-85.

Bergquist, W. 1993. Post Modern Thought in a Nutshell. [Published in *Classics of Organization Theory* (4th Edition – J. Shafritz and J. Ott, editors), New York: Harcourt Brace College Publishers, 1996. Adapted from Bergquist, W. 1993. *The Postmodern Organization: Mastering the Art of Irreversible Change*, Jossey-Bass Inc., Publishers, pp. 15-36.]

Boghossian, P. 2006. *Fear of Knowledge: Against Relativism and Constructivism*. Oxford: Oxford University Press.

Dedvedzic, V. 2002. Understanding Ontological Engineering. *Communications of the ACM* 45(4):136-144.

Ferrario, R. and N. Guardino. 2008. Towards an Ontological Foundation for Services Science. *Proceedings of the Future Internet Symposium,* Vienna Austria, 28-30 September 2008.

Fitzsimmons, J.A. and M.J. Fitzsimmons. 2006. *Service Management: Operations, Strategy, Information Technology* (5th Edition), New York: McGraw-Hill Irwin.

Gruber, T. 2008. Ontology. *Encyclopedia of Database Systems,* Liu, L. and M. Ozsu (Eds.), Springer-Verlag,

Guarino, N. 1995. Formal Ontology, Conceptual Analysis and Knowledge Representation. *International Journal of Human-Computer Studies,* 43(5-6):907-928.

IBM Almaden Services Research. 2006. "SSME: What are services?" Referenced from the following Web site: http://almaden.ibm.com/ssme.

Katzan, H. 2008a. Event Differentiation in Service Science. *Journal of Business and Economics Research,* 6(5): 141-152.

Katzan, H. 2008b. *Service Science: Concepts, Technology, Management.* New York: iUniverse, Inc.

Kuhn, T. 1996. *The Structure of Scientific Revolution* (3rd edition), Chicago: University of Chicago Press. [Secondary reference]

Maglio, P. and J. Zysman. 2007. Toward a Science of Service Systems. *Sofcon 2007.* Carnegie Mellon University, April 30, 2007, pp. 5-6.

Newell, A., Perlis, A., and H.A. Simon. 1967. Computer Science. *Science,* 157: 1373-1374. [Secondary reference]

Sampson, S. and C. Froehle. 2006. Foundations and Implications of a Proposed Unified Services Theory. *Productions and Operations Management,* 15(2): 329-343.

Selznick, P. 1948. Foundations of the Theory of Organization. *American Sociological Review* 13: 25-35. [Published in *Classics of Organization Theory* (4th Edition – J. Shafritz and J. Ott, editors), New York: Harcourt Brace College Publishers, 1996.]

Smith, A. 1776. *The Wealth of Nations,* published as "An Inquiry into the Nature and Causes of the Wealth of Nations" in London, England (1776).

Sowa, J. 2000. *Knowledge Representation: Logical, Philosophical and Computational Foundations,* Brooks Cole Publishing.

Spohrer, J., Anderson, L., Pass, N., Ager, T., and D. Gruhl. 2007a. Service Science. *Journal of Grid Computing* (Special Issue of Grid Economics and Business Models, August 2, 2007).

Spohrer. J., Vargo, S., Caswell, N., and P. Maglio. 2007b. The Service System is the Basic Abstraction of Service Science. IBM Almaden Research Center, http://www.almaden.ibm.com/asr.

Sutherland, J. 1975. *Systems: Analysis, Administration, and Architecture.* New York: Van Nostrand Reinhold Co.

Wikipedia. 2009. Ontology, www.wikipedia.org/ontology.

Toward a Unified Ontology of Trusted Identity

The nation's digital infrastructure is in jeopardy because of inadequate provisions for privacy, identity, and security. The "everyone is free to do everything" mentally that would appear to be prevalent in America and worldwide has resulted in an onslaught of identity theft, fraud, digital crime, and an unnecessary concern over cyber security by many individuals. It is patently necessary for careful participants to operate defensively in cyberspace in order to protect themselves from the evils just mentioned. Those that do not act responsibly do so at their own peril. In fact, digital crime has served as a precursor to and is associated with physical crime. (OECD 2008)

The computer security and Internet communities have been generally responsive but apparently ineffective, so it is time for a third party to step in, take charge, and provide an infrastructure to assist in protecting the citizens of the world. (White House 2010) Similar concerns prevail in other developed countries, since many cyber crimes are perpetrated from lesser-developed countries without cyber awareness from legal, political, economic, and technical perspectives. Moreover, there are no good reasons why underdeveloped countries should get a free-ride in this regard.

The nations and organizations that lend a blind-eye to its residents that commit cyber-crimes against persons and organizations in other countries will change their tune when cyber benefits are subsequently denied to them through political, social, and technological processes.

This paper is a contribution to the domain of **ontological** commitment as it applies to a description of subjects, objects, actions, and relationships as they pertain to the National Strategy of Trusted Identity in Cyberspace initiative.

BASIC CONCEPTS

Identity is a major issue in the security of modern information systems and the privacy of data stored in those systems. Identity and privacy concerns are commonly associated with behavioral tracking, personal-identifiable information (PII), the relevance of private data, data repurposing, and identity theft. (Windley 2005) We are going to approach the subject from an information systems perspective, recognizing that the inherent problems also apply to societal systems. Information systems are a good conceptual vehicle for the underlying security, identity, and privacy models, because data is typically stored off-premises and is under the control of a third-party service provider. When a third party gets your data, who knows what is going to happen to it? The main consideration may turn out to be a matter of control, because from an organizational perspective, control over information has historically been with the organization that creates or maintains it. From a personal perspective, on the other hand, persons should

have the wherewithal to control their identity and the release of information about themselves, and in the latter case, a precise determination of to whom it is released and for what reason. Privacy issues are not fundamentally caused by technology, but they are exacerbated by employing the technology for economic benefit. After a brief review of identity and privacy to set the stage, we are going to cover identity theory, privacy theory, and identity requirements. This is a working paper on this important subject.

Identity

Identity is a means of denoting an entity in a particular namespace and is the basis of security and privacy – regardless if the context is digital identification or non-digital identification. We are going to refer to an identity object as a *subject*. A subject may have several identities and belong to more than one namespace. An identity denotation is based on attributes as suggested by Figure 1.

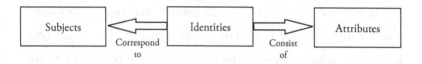

Figure 1. Conceptual relationship between
subjects, identities, and attributes.

A pure identity denotation is independent of a specific context, and a federated identity reflects a process that is shared between identity management systems. When one identity management system accepts the certification of another, a phenomenon known

as "trust" is established. The execution of trust is often facilitated by a third party that is acknowledged by both parties and serves as the basis of digital identity in information systems.

Access to computing facilities is achieved through a process known as authentication, whereby an entity makes a claim to its identity by presenting an identity symbol for verification and control. Authentication is usually paired with a related specification known as authorization to obtain the right to address a given service.

It is generally felt that a framework for understanding a technology should reflect the underlying concepts required for its development and subsequent acceptance as an operational modality. A technology should enable the delivery of value rather than constrain it, and that is our objective with this paper.

Privacy

Information systems typically process and store information about which privacy is of paramount concern. The main issue is identity, which serves as the basis of privacy or lack of it, and undermines the trust of individuals and organizations in other information-handling entities. The key consideration may turn out to be the integrity that organizations display when handling personal information and how accountable they are about their information practices. From an organizational perspective, control over information should remain with the end user or the data's creator with adequate controls over repurposing. From a personal

perspective, the person should have the wherewithal to control his or her identity as well as the release of socially sensitive identity attributes. One of the beneficial aspects of the present concern over information privacy is that it places the person about whom data are recorded in proper perspective. Whereas such a person may be the object in an information system, he or she is regarded as the subject in privacy protection – as mentioned earlier. This usage of the word *subject* is intended to imply that a person should, in fact, have some control over the storage of personal information.

More specifically, the *subject* is the person, natural or legal, about whom data is stored. The *beneficial user* is the organization or individual for whom processing is performed, and the *agency* is the computing system in which the processing is performed and information is stored. In many cases, the beneficial user and the subject are members of the same organization.

The heart of the issue is *privacy protection*, which normally refers to the protection of rights of individuals. While the concept may also apply to groups of individuals, the individual aspect of the issue is that which raises questions of privacy and liberty

Privacy Assessment

The Federal Bureau of Investigation (U.S.A.) lists several criteria for evaluating privacy concerns for individuals and for designing computer applications: (FBI 2004)

- *What information is being collected?*

- *Why is the information being collected?*
- *What is the intended use of the information?*
- *With whom will the information be shared?*
- *What opportunities will individuals have to decline to provide information or to consent to particular uses of the information?*
- *How will the information be secure?*
- *Is this a system of records?*

Since privacy is a fundamental right in the United States, the above considerations obviously resulted from extant concerns by individuals and privacy rights groups. In a 2009 Legislative Primer, the following concerns are expressed by the Center for Digital Democracy: (CDD 2009, p. 2)

- Tracking people's every move online is an invasion of privacy.
- Online behavioral tracking and targeting can be used to take advantage of vulnerable consumers.
- Online behavioral tracking and targeting can be used to unfairly discriminate against consumers.
- Online behavioral profiles may be used for purposes beyond commercial purposes.

We are going to add to the list that the very fact that personal data is stored online is a matter of concern and should be given serious attention. Based on these issues, this paper is going to take a comprehensive look at the subject of identity in computer and human systems.

IDENTITY THEORY

The notion of identity is an important subject in philosophy, mathematics, and computer information systems. In its most general sense, identity refers to the set of characteristics that makes a subject definable. Each characteristic can be viewed as a single point in a three-dimensional Cartesian coordinate system where the axis are *subject, attribute,* and *value.* (Katzan 1975) Thus, the fact that George is twenty-five years old could be denoted by the triple <George, age, 25>. A set of characteristics over a given domain can uniquely identify a subject. This simple concept is the basis of privacy and identity in information systems and everyday life. The notion of identity applies to organizational subjects as well as to person subjects.

Knowledge, Attributes, and Identity

Identity is primarily used to establish a relationship between an attribute or set of attributes and a person, object, event, concept, or theory. The relationship can be direct, based on physical evidence, and in other cases, the relationship is indirect and based on a reference to other entities. In a similar vein, the relationship can be certain or uncertain, and in the latter case, based in deduction or inference. The relationship determines an element of knowledge. For example, the knowledge element "you are in your car" is a statement in which "you" and "your car" are things that exist and the "in" is a relationship. Direct knowledge is known by *acquaintance* and is evidenced by a physical connection. Indirect knowledge is determined through a reference to a particular with

which the analyst is acquainted. The form is known as knowledge by *description*. (Russell 1912) *Direct knowledge* is determined through sense data, memory, or introspection. *Indirect knowledge* is determined through a reference to another particular, as in "the person who ran for Congress in 2004" or through a form of self-awareness where what goes on in subject's mind, for example, is estimated by an analyst's interpretation based on experience or self-evaluation.

Synthetic knowledge reflects certainty based on evidence inherent in the attribute values at hand. *Analytic knowledge* reflects a degree of uncertainty and is determined by deduction, as in "he is the only person with that 'attribute value'," or by inference based on known particulars, such as "all terrorists have beards." Inference, in this case, could be regarded as a form of derivative knowledge. The value of analytic knowledge is that it enables the analyst to exceed his or her limit of private experience.

Numerical and Qualitative Identity

Identity refers to the characteristics that make a subject the same or different. We are going to establish two forms of identity: numerical and qualitative. Two subjects are *numerically identical* if they are the same entity, such that there is only one instance. Two subject (or objects in this case) are *qualitatively identical* if they are copies or duplicates. In the popular movie *The Bourne Identity*, for example, the characters *Jason Bourne* and *David Web* are numerically identical, and the number of subjects is one. So it is with *Superman* and *Clark Kent* in another domain. On the other

hand, a set of animals with the same biological characteristics – e.g., a species – are regarded as being qualitatively identical. The notion of qualitative identity is remarkably similar to the modern definition of a *category* informally defined as a collection of entities with the same characteristics, having the same values for the same attributes.

Theory of the Indiscernibles

An important aspect of identity theory is that subjects exhibit features of permanence and change, analogous to sameness and difference mentioned previously. We are going to discuss the concept of temporal identity in the next section. The notion of change implies that a subject undergoes transformation and also has a property that remains unchanged. Both Locke and Hume have proclaimed that change reflects the idea of unity and not of identity. Leibnitz proposed the *Theory of Indiscernibles* suggesting that subjects (i.e., objects or entities) that are indiscernible are identical. (Stroll 1967) The subject of indiscernibles has implications for information systems and attribute change. To what extent a change in a characteristic denotes a change in identity is an open item at this time and implies that there is a probabilistic aspect to identity.

Russell approaches the subject of identity from an alternate viewpoint, analogous to definite and indefinite articles. Russell proposes that a description may be of two sorts: definite and indefinite. A definite description is a name, and an indefinite description is a collection of objects x that have the property ø,

such that the proposition øx is true. (Russell 1919) In the phrase *Dan Brown is a famous author*, for example, 'Dan Brown" is a name and the indefinite description is obvious, leading to the probabilistic link between a subject and a characteristic.

Temporal Identity

There is a rich quantity of philosophical literature on the change of identity over time. Are you the same person you were yesterday? Are there persistent attributes that allow for positive identity between time periods? As alluded to previously, entities in everyday life exhibit features of permanence and change. In the domain of personal identity, address attribute is a primary candidate for change. For example, John Smith lives at 123 Main Street. He moves out and another John Smith moves in. This is a distinct possibility in a crowded city. In there a concept in identity theory for this phenomena? Should an identity system take this eventuality into consideration?

There is a form of *attribute duality* between a person subject and an object subject. A subject – an object, such as a residence, in this case – is characterized by who lives there. For example, rich people live on Sutton Place in New York. The discussion leads to four related concepts: endurant identity, perdurant identity, endurant attribute, and perdurant attribute. Clearly, the term *endurant* refers to a noun that does not change, where perdurant refers to one that does. Thus, the identity problem is essentially translated to an operant problem of "recognizing identity."

PRIVACY THEORY

It has long been recognized that privacy is a two-edged sword, not only for individuals, but also for groups and organizations. Subjects have First and Fourth Amendment rights designed to protect against unwarranted disclosure of information with unlimited scope to unwanted parties without proper authorization by the subject. However, privacy considerations protect criminals and terrorists, in addition to ordinary citizens, groups, and organizations. Protections and other conventions used to safeguard trade secrets can also be employed to enable non-disclosure of design and manufacturing flaws from consumers and regulatory bodies.

Privacy has been in the news for at least forty years originating with Alan Westin's seminal book on the subject entitled *Privacy and Freedom,* published in 1967. Others have joined the struggle, namely (Westin 1977, Miller 1971, Katzan 1980, and Givens 2009) to reference only a few of many, with apologies to those not mentioned. One of the toughest problems facing the computer industry is data protection, summarized very well in 1971 by Arthur R. Miller: (Miller 1971, p.37)

> The new information technologies seem to have given birth to a new social virus – "data-mania." Its symptoms are shortness of breath and heart palpitations when contemplating a new computer application, a feeling of possessiveness about

information and a deep resentment toward those who won't yield it, a delusion that all information handlers can walk on water, and a highly advanced case of astigmatism that prevents the affected victim from perceiving anything but the intrinsic value of data. Fortunately, only some members of the information-handling fraternity have been stricken by the disease.

This quote was written over 39 years ago; what would the author think about today's environment?

Privacy and Data Protection

Data protection is given the most attention when the privacy of an individual or an organization is jeopardized. According to Alan F. Westin: (Westin 1967)

Privacy is the claim of individuals, groups, or institutions to determine for themselves when, how, and to what extent information about them is communicated to others.

Privacy is related to data protection, because it is an integral part of society and affects the behavior of its citizens. *Privacy is a service that a subject should expect from and be provided by society.* The physical state of being private has four primary attributes: solitude, intimacy, anonymity, and reserve, which supply group separation, group participation, group freedom,

and personal protection, respectively. These states collectively provide the confidentiality required to participate in a civilized society. Concerns for privacy should be an integral part of a data protection program.

An organization requires privacy to achieve its basic objective – whether it is business, education, or government. The disclosure of private internal affairs affects "brand equity" and is detrimental to success.

Another consideration is personal surveillance – even though it may be socially or legally accepted. When a subject does not have control over its informational profile, there is no safeguard over its authenticity. Therefore, a double barreled approach, consisting of technology and regulation, is required for operating in a global economy. (Katzan, 1980, p. 44)

Information Control

Because of the widespread application of computer and communications technology, there has been a gradual trend among private institutions and government agencies to ignore the individual's need for privacy. Privacy safeguards are the individual's sole line of defense against the exercise of power through information control. Individuals can lose control of information about themselves in three ways:

1. Information obtained against the subject's wishes.

2. Information obtained from an agency against the wishes of the agency and of the subject.

3. Information willingly disclosed by the beneficial user or agency but against the subject's wishes.

Information obtained against a subject's wishes is an area in which privacy is normally expected. This category includes explicit attempts to obtain information and implicit methods where a subject is forced to disclose personal information. Typical actions are:

1. Searches and seizure
2. Compelled self-disclosure
3. Informers and secret agents
4. Participant monitoring
5. Public observation and recording of information
6. Consent for fear of reprisal
7. Disclosure for privilege

Some benefits are commonly associated with disclosure of private information, so the fine line between willing and unauthorized disclosure is frequently blurred. In the case of *Information obtained from an agency against the wishes of the agency and of the subject*, the conditions of privacy should apply to the agency as they do to the subject and are normally of concern because of computer security deficiencies and unauthorized access. In the case of *Information willingly disclosed by the beneficial user or agency but against the subject's wishes*, as in interagency transfers, accuracy and context are normally of concern. This

is the prototypical *repurposing of information* that lies at the heart of most subjects' concerns over the disclosure of personal information.

Recordkeeping

Records typically fall into four classes: administrative, operational, intelligence, and statistical. In theory, *administrative records* are maintained by governmental agencies and give subjects their identity. For individuals, administrative records normally include birth certificates, diplomas, military discharge papers, driver's licenses, and immigration papers. For organizations, administrative records include certificates of incorporation and related documents. *Operational records* reflect tax and other certificates. *Intelligence records* are maintained by government agencies and represent security permissions and legal investigations. *Statistical records* can be obtained through an official questionnaire, as with the census, or from any of the other records that have been "cleansed" so as not to reflect personal information. Privacy safeguards are summarized in a far-reaching report by the Department of Health, Education, and Welfare (HEW 1973, pp. xx-xxi.):

1. There must be no personal data record-keeping systems whose very existence is secret.
2. There must be a way for an individual to find out what information about him is in a record and how it is used.
3. There must be a way for an individual to prevent information about him that was obtained for one purpose

from being used or made available for other purposes without his consent.

4. There must be a way for an individual to correct or amend a record of identifiable information about him.

5. Any organization creating, maintaining, using, or disseminating records of identifiable personal data must assure the reliability of the data for their intended use and must take precautions to prevent misuse of the data.

The five principles are regarded as a Code of Fair Information Practice, emphasizing that privacy is a service that should be afforded to all citizens by other citizens, organizations, and the government in a free and open society.

Privacy Issues

The subject of privacy in all of its "multi-faceted dimensions" is of concern to many persons. Some individuals only wake up to the subject when their privacy is invaded and then quickly go back to sleep when the situation subsides, or they get tired of worrying about it. In the present context, Internet computing would seem to constitute a privacy threat to many persons and also organizations, because sensitive information is held by third-party service providers. However, having a third-party service provider is not a necessary condition for privacy invasion. The gang-of-three (government, employers, and education) would appear to be doing a good job with that. What are the specific issues about which we should be concerned? The topic has been addressed by the Privacy Rights Clearinghouse (PRC) in a document entitled

"Privacy Today: A Review of Current Issues" developed by its director Dr. Beth Givens. (Givens 2009) The report lists twenty-three issues in privacy rights with a substantial description of each issue. The report highlights and summarizes the key issues and also contains links to special interest groups working on particular topics in that domain. We are going to concentrate on five subjects deemed relevant to the mission of this compendium:

- Biometrics
- Video surveillance and workplace monitoring
- Data profiling
- Behavioral tracking and targeting
- Records on the Internet

A selection from the PRC list is also necessary because every privacy subject has its privacy point and twenty-three primary issues are more than we can usefully cover in this paper. Here is a simple straight-forward case of an individual personal privacy concern. "Joe Smith is a good runner and ran a local marathon in 3 hours and 20 minutes. The marathon organizer lists the name, age, finishing time, finisher's place, and home city and state of all finishers of the race on the Web. Joe has two concerns. He is a bit embarrassed, because a couple of years ago, he ran the same race in less than 3 hours. So, in this case Joe would prefer not to have the results published online for everyone to see – that is, if anyone besides runners would be interested. Joe's friend Al has a different opinion. Al says, 'That is a great time Joe. My father, who is about your age, ran it in 3 hours and 10 minutes.' The second concern is more serious. Joe is 57 years old and is looking for a good position,

since he was recently laid off. He is concerned that a prospective employer can Google him and determine his age from the online list of finishers, since age discrimination is a major concern for many employers in this country." If the race were run in Canada or Europe, on the other hand, the same information would not be available to outside persons, because of privacy laws.

We are going to present a descriptive technique that will apply the five selected dimensions, placing each dimension in a privacy-identity continuum.

Biometrics

The term *biometrics* refers to the use of bodily characteristics for identification, which can be exact or probabilistic. If you have been in the ROTC, the military, law enforcement, possess a government security clearance, or have been born recently, you have an exact biometric identity consisting of your set of fingerprints on file in an official place. A person's DNA and retinal scan are also supposedly exact biometric identifiers. Clearly, an exact biometric marking does in fact identify a particular individual. However, the assignment of a name from an appropriate namespace is quite another thing. If the task is to link an individual with a specific name, then there is some probability involved. The picture on an official passport, driver's license, or government issued identification is also regarded as an exact identifier. But, how exact is exact? As mentioned before, there is some risk in linking name identification between two or more types of identity.

Less exact biometrics, such as facial recognition, has been employed in social situations to identify persons of interest – such as at sporting events. Using facial geometry and other visual clues, facial recognition technology has been very successful in criminal investigation. But, what about the identification and recording of persons in a lawful demonstration, guaranteed as a First Amendment right? Everyone knows there are at least two kind of demonstrators: those persons participating in the physical part of a demonstration because they genuinely believe in the cause, and those persons with nothing else to do on a Saturday afternoon. As Dr. Givens writes, "As a result, innocent people can be wrongly identified as criminal (false-positives), and known criminal and suspected terrorists can fail to be detected altogether (false-negatives).

Video Surveillance and Workplace Monitoring

Low-cost video surveillance systems are prevalent in modern society, and their use ranges from convenience stores to day-care centers. In fact, video surveillance is so pervasive that most people think nothing about being under the eye of the camera. In criminal investigation, video surveillance is a useful identifier, albeit within some probabilistic limits, and also as an investigative tool.

Collectively, video surveillance and workplace monitoring can provide information related to the following phenomena:

- Facial recognition

- Unproductive employment activity
- Improper use of resources
- Violation of conditions of service

Use of an employer's computer or other resources is a good case in point. There are other forms of surveillance, such as Radio Frequency Identification (RFID) chips embedded in employee identification cards that can be used as an employee locator by recording when he or she leaves one room and enters another.

Keystroke monitors are sometimes used to determine ineffective use of equipment. Most employees do not seem to mind employee monitoring when on premises – but what can they do about it? Off premises and off hours surveillance and monitoring are quite another thing and exist as an open issue in privacy.

Data Profiling

Most of us are well represented in a multitude of gang-of-three databases, such as the tax bureau, social security administration, state motor vehicles office, education records, employment files, insurance, and health records. Information of this type can be regarded as the operational part of the fabric of life. We can temper the intrusion but not totally eliminate it, because it is paramount to identity determination and service management. Identities are linked by numbers, such as the social-security number, name, date of birth, telephone number, address and ZIP code, mother's maiden name, and even mother's birthday. It

is even possible to find the social security number of an unrelated deceased person on the Web. Immigration records are also easily obtainable. The Privacy Act of 1974 and its amendments generally cover governmental data protection and profiling.

There is another form of data that is involuntarily collected about individuals where there is some choice involved, such as personal expenditures, lifestyle, Internet activity, political activity and donations, and so forth. Supermarkets, bookstores, department stores, health stores, fitness centers, libraries, toll booths, big-ticket retailers, travel agencies, magazine publishers, and airlines – all contain personal data on individuals. An idea of interests, activities, and expenditures are available from credit card purchases, bank records, and operational files of business, governmental, and educational institutions. Thus, it is quite easy for an interested party to create a *data profile* of a person.

Pundits claim that profile data determines who or what we are. However, there is a tendency to interpret data based on the psychological perspective of the profiler. If you subscribe to "guns and ammo," does that indicate that you are a terrorist, member of the local shooting club, an Olympic athlete, worker in a sporting goods store that sells guns, or a medical professional who uses a service to provide magazines for the waiting room.

It has been reported that search providers turn over search queries of individuals to the agencies of the government. (Conti 2009, pp.259-298) This is a modern form of data profiling. A method, termed *chaffing,* is mentioned to widen the search

domain and provide some protection. So, if you are going to search for a controversial person, you might also want to search for some non-threatening person to widen the search area.

Behavioral Tracking and Targeting

`Behavioral tracking and targeting is an area of privacy concern related to data profiling with emphasis on what a subject does. Here is a typical scenario. A subject rents a car and drives that vehicle out of state or out of the country by accident or by intention. When the car is turned in to the agency, the renter is charged an enormous penalty. The fine print in the contract was not read, because the renter is usually out of his or her element or just in a hurry. How did the agency know of the unfortunate travel? The car rental agency used a global positioning system (GPS) device to track the path of the vehicle. In addition to GPS tracking, license plate tracking, implemented through highway cameras, is also widely used by state and local law enforcement officials. There is always a stated reason why organizations do things, but in the case of privacy, the main problem is the repurposing of collected data. Through data mining technology, computers can identify patterns based on happenstance, rather than purposeful activity. Here is another example: At the time this paragraph was written, the state of Arizona decided to take border control into its own hands. The federal government could do it and can do it, but we live in a large country with enough problems to go around. Getting the right person's or an organization's attention at the right time usually takes some up front planning. Demonstrations

ensue for varying reasons, including the possibility that certain outside people want to stir up trouble. Proper officials are looking into persons flying into Arizona with recently booked tickets for travel lasting only a few days and are doing some data mining to identify those persons. Are identified persons demonstration instigators or grandparents attending a graduation ceremony. Regardless, they are prime candidates for behavioral tracking. In an era of supercomputing, piecing together a travel itinerary is not a major task. All that is needed is a subject to track.

The subject of behavioral tracking also includes the practice of collecting and compiling consumers' online activities, interests, preferences, and/or communications over time. (Givens 2009, 18 of 23) This form of behavioral targeting serves as the basis for advertising and other forms of marketing. Web browsing is a primary source of information in this regard.

There is also a growing trend by Internet service providers (ISPs) to use deep packet investigation (DPI) to look at email, Web sites visited, music, video sharing, and downloads by inspecting the data packets that constitute Internet traffic. This form of privacy intrusion is a major challenge to privacy advocates.

Records on the Internet

There is a tendency in society for persons in a political or geographical jurisdiction to be generally the same. This refers to attitudes, culture, psychological properties, and so forth. Between countries, however, there tend to be some differences between the

two groups of people. People from Switzerland are different from people from England. The same idea holds true for people from Minnesota and Georgia, for example. We are referring to what is acceptable behavior, from a cultural viewpoint, or "would you like that person living next door."

The disclosure of public records in an open government is not sensitive to cultural differences, since the context for the information in government-managed files does not travel with the information. Citizens in one area may be more or less sensitive to the content of public information than persons from another – especially in a large country. The "one size fits all" mentality of public disclosure is a subject that frustrates privacy advocates.

Nevertheless, divorce records, criminal records, under-age convictions, bankruptcy proceedings, DIU convictions, motor vehicle records, and so forth, are all publically available through mailing list and information brokers. All an identity thief or stalker needs is a Social Security number and $19.95. The motivation for many, if not most, automobile breakins in modern times is an attempt to obtain personal information in the glove box, even thought the thief may also take a camera from the rear seat.

IDENTITY REQUIREMENTS

It would appear that there are two essential problems in identity theory: protection of identity and recognition of identity. Protection refers to the safeguarding of one's identity from unwanted intrusion into personal affairs, and is reflected

in the identity principles that follow. Recognition refers to the use of identity measures to classify certain persons, based on the combination of evidence and abductive inference. This characterization of the identity problem reflects two edges of the same sword.

Identity Principles

It is generally regarded that effective identity governance should be based on a set of principles to guide the professional activities of IT managers, security officers, privacy officers, and risk management. (Salido 2010, OECD 2010) As delineated, the principles would be based on efficacy in governance, risk management, and compliance with the following objectives:

> **Governance.** Assurance that the organization focuses on basic issues and who is responsible for actions and outcomes.

> **Risk Management.** Assurance that procedures are in place for identifying, analyzing, evaluating, remedying, and monitoring risk.

> **Compliance.** Assurance that actions are within the scope of social and legal provisions.

In accordance with the stated objectives, we can delineate the eight core principles of effective and efficient identity management. (OECD op cit., p.3)

Principle #1. Collection Limitation Principle – there should be prudent limits on the collection of personal data with the knowledge or consent of the subject.

Principle #2. Data Quality Principle – personal data should be relevant to stated purposes and be accurate, complete, and up-to-date.

Principle #3. Purpose Specification Principle – the purpose of the data collection should be specified beforehand.

Principle #4. Use Limitation Principle – data should be used only for the use specified and not be repurposed.

Principle #5. Security Safeguards Principle – personal data should be safeguarded by reasonable and state-of-the art security facilities.

Principle #6. Openness Principle – the technical infrastructure for protecting personal data should be open as to development, practices, and policies.

Principle #7. Individual Participation Principle – the subject should have the right to definitive information concerning the personal data collected, methods used, and safeguards employed

and have the right to challenge the procedures employed.

Principle #8. Accountability Principle – social, business, educational, and governmental data controllers should be required by legal or regularity means to abide by principles 1-8 and be accountable for violations of their provisions.

The eight principles of identity agree in part and parcel to Cavoukian's "7 Laws of Identity, listed as follows: personal control and consent; minimal disclosure for limited use; need to know access; user-directed identity; universal monitoring of the use of identification technology; human understanding and involvement; and consistent access and interface to personal data. (Cavoukian 2010)

Identity Analytics

An important aspect of identity theory concerns whether a certain subject is a member of a group of interest. The basis for this form of identity determination is that identity is a function of the subject's namespace and attributes. A subject belongs to a category if it possesses the attributes that define the category. Another approach is to employ a knowledge source to determine a subject's group membership. This is the method we are going to use in this section. A popular characterization of the problem would be, "Is suspect A a member of group T?" or in short form, "Is A a T?" Clearly, the methods would apply to most diagnostic

systems, such as medical diagnosis, auto repair, and the analysis of aircraft failures. We are going to propose two methods of analysis: the combination of evidence (Shafer 1976, Katzan 2006, Katzan 2010) and abductive inference (Josephson 1996).

With the *combination of evidence*, a certain level of belief is afforded a knowledge source, as in the following scenario:

> *We are trying to identify subjects that belong to a certain group G. We know about the group G and its attributes. We have a paid knowledge source K_1 that informs us that subject A is a member of G. However, K_1 is not always correct, and we know that. We have used K_1 enough to know that he provides us with information when he needs money. We have an intuitive belief of how often he is correct. Fortunately, we have another source K_2 that can supply similar information. K_2 is not as hungry for money as K_1, and his opinion frequently runs contrary to K_1's. We would like to use analytics to combine the information from K_1 and K_2 so as to obtain a composite picture of the situation.*

The relations between the knowledge sources and the subject are represented by the following mappings:

$$K_1 \rightarrow A$$
$$K_2 \rightarrow A$$

and the characteristics of the relationships are given as:

$$A = \{m, n\}$$
$$K_1 = \{r, u\}$$
$$K_2 = \{c, i\}$$

The question is whether A is a member of G, denoted by m, or not a member of G, denoted by n. As far as K_1 is concerned, he might be telling us what he thinks we want to hear, so his judgment is classed as reliable, denoted by r, or unreliable, denoted by u. K_2 is simply correct or incorrect, denoted by c or i, respectively. Through a method known as belief propagation (Katzan 2010a), the knowledge is transferred from the problem space to the solution space, resulting in the following representation:

Source	Representation
K_1	$\{[(m), p].\ [(m, n), 1\text{-}p]\}$
K_2	$\{[(n), q].\ [(m, n), 1\text{-}q]\}$

The results of belief propagation assign the mass (p) of the information received from K_1 to (m) and the remainder of the belief is assigned to (m, n). A similar argument applies to K_2 such that the mass (q) of that belief is assigned to (n) and the remainder to (m, n). Using Dempster's rules of combination (Dempster 1967), the resulting forms can be combined yielding the following assessment in the solution space:

$$\left[(m), \frac{p(1-q)}{1-pq}\right], \left[(n), \frac{(1-p)q}{1-pq}\right], \left[(m,n), \frac{(1-p)(1-q)}{1-pq}\right]$$

using symbolic math from calculations in *Mathematica*™. Applying the expression to several values of p and q yields the following results:

K_1 (p)	K_2 (q)	$K_1 \oplus K_2$
.6	.7	{[(m), 0.310], [(n), 0.483], [(m, n), 0.207]}
.7	.5	{[(m), 0.538], [(n), 0.231], [(m, n), 0.231]}

This is what we wanted to show. QED.

An alternate methodology, known as *abductive inference*, is used to determine the probable cause of group membership. (Josephson 1996) As with many forms of diagnosis, we have an event or condition and wish to determine the probable cause of the occurrence. A person may have a condition, such as liver disease, or a physical system may fail, such as a fighter aircraft. The list of probable causes in each instance is called the *differential*. Abductive inference is often referred to as, "turning modus ponens induction on its head." Abduction takes the following pattern:

E is an event or a collection of data

C explains E

No other hypothesis can explain E and well as C

--

Therefore, C is probably true

For example, J attends a training camp that is associated with membership in a militant group. There could be several possible causes for this phenomenon, two of which are that J is a militant

or wants to be one. J could also be a journalist wanting to find out about things, but that is definitely less probable. The use of subjective probabilities, assigned through abductive inference, can be an analytic technique in its own right, or it can be used as input to a "combination of evidence" methodology.

Abductive inference and consensus theory would appear to be promising research topics for the modern world.

SUMMARY

Personal identity and privacy are important topics in the modern world of communications and the Internet. Most citizens are not aware of the major issues or do not realize the serious nature of identity theft and privacy invasion. The academic community is needed to foster attention to this subject, and this paper attempts to spotlight the major concerns. Accordingly, this paper is an admixture of topics that include identity, identity theory, privacy, and privacy theory, along with a summary of the major aspects of each domain. There is due consideration given to identity requirements through a set of identity principles and some proposals for identity analytics. In the latter instance, evidential methods are presented as promising research topics.

REFERENCES

1. ACLU of Northern California. 2010. *Cloud Computing: Storm Warning for Privacy?* www.dotrights.org, (downloaded 3/11/2010).

2. Black, M. 1952. Identity of Indiscernibles. *Mind* 61:153. (Secondary reference.)

3. Cavoukian, A. 2009. *Privacy in the Clouds.* Toronto: Information and Privacy Commission of Ontario (www. ipc.on.ca).

4. Cavoukian, A. 2010. 7 Laws of Identity: The Case for Privacy-Embedded Laws of Identity I the Digital Age." Toronto: Information and Privacy Commission of Ontario (www.ipc.on.ca).

5. Katzan, H. 2010. *Privacy, Identity, and Cloud Computing,* New York: iUniverse, Inc.

6. OECD 2010. OECD Guidelines on the Protection of Privacy and Transborder Flows of Personal Data. www. oecd.org. (downloaded 3/23/2010).

7. Salido, J. and P. Voon. 2010. A Guide to Data Governance for Privacy, Confidentiality, and Compliance: Part 1. The Case for Data Governance. Microsoft Corporation.

Recent Developments in Artificial Intelligence Ontology

It is possible to summarize the current state of the art in Modern Artificial Intelligence in one paragraph, followed by more definitive information, as required. Most of the activity is taking place in universities and small companies. The only big gun in the area is IBM that has incredible experience in research, engineering, and marketing. This doesn't mean that there isn't intelligent and experienced people working on it, but when we get down to business, artificial intelligence is a service to mankind and experience goes a long way. There is a tremendous amount of hype surrounding generative AI. Organizations of all sizes are rushing to control the transformative possibilities and the marketing potential. Generative AI will used to enhance large language models to power subsequent generative AI. Capabilities in the following categories will be required to leverage AI: language and image related capability, natural language processing, document understanding, capability of content search, summarization, and system augmentation. In order to streamline tasks and processes, efficient and advanced decision making are required. Things will have to be done differently in the following areas: quantity and quality of data, domain specific models, high quality data processing, the use of the best technologies, and the use of

automated business processes. Jobs of tomorrow will be different and the manner in which people work and their skill set will be different. Narrowly defined jobs will be modified through hybrid and remote work. Employee experience will be key and a high percentage of job descriptions haven not yet be defined.

Ontology Knowledge Models

In the future, AI systems will be used to enhance their very selves. This will be achieved through machine learning and through the use of ontologies to delineate new systems. A knowledge base will be used to store the ontologies and machine learning data and that knowledge will be codified as:

Object -> Thesaurus -> Taxonomy

Often, a parent/child relationship will exist of the following form:

Equivalence -> Hierarchical -> Associative

An ontology will be used to represent a total application. An AI system will probably use many AI projects, that will be established with marketable software. With AI, this is supposed to be done by the development software that analyzes the application domain and yields an operational system.

There aren't many situations that exist to serve as an explanatory model. One of the recent books on the concept us *The AI-Powered Enterprise: Harness the Powers of Ontologies to*

Make Your Business Smarter, Faster, and More Profitable, authored by Seth Early, the founder and CEO of an early third-generation AI application on the subject.

Data Ontology

A data ontology is a method for listing a collection of elements with different structures. Data ontologies are a means of organizing data. A data ontology describes a structure and not values.

Semantic Web

In a semantic web, the data elements of concern have a "collected" structure with an inherent flexibility in contrast to a set of database tables and facilitative vocabularies, taxonomies, thesauruses, maps, logic models, and conventional databases. A semantic web provides human readable data.

A data ontology is used to organize data for a particular application domain.

Ontology Advantages

A data ontology provides a description of data elements and their relationships and reflects the structure of an AI system. Accordingly, a data ontology performs like a human brain – at least, that at least one mode of reserve contends. Examples are not readable available.

Deep Learning

The use of an ontology structure facilitates four types of learning in an AI application: deep learning, supervised machine learning, unsupervised machine learning, and a reinforcement machine learning. There is a form of organization inherent in the structure of the various components:

AI system -> Machine learning -> Deep learning

With data science interacting with data elements of all three areas.

A Look at the Future

There is a large number of universities, scientific labs, large companies, and start-ups in the general area of artificial intelligence. Each organization has its own point of view and an organization desiring to use advanced AI for a serious form of operation. What is needed is to have the resources to lead the way. The situation is similar to the large computer industry – called the mainframes – where the business atmosphere would have been in total chaos had it not been for the foresight of IBM and its direct marketing.

I the current environment, that would be the case with artificial intelligence. Therein lies the reason for this book. Every application domain has its own needs. Clearly, abank, insurance company, automobile company and so forth cannot have the

capability of developing core AI systems, but they should possess the core internal knowledge about what is going on.

Generative Artificial Intelligence is a service business with all rights, privileges, and advantages pertaining thereto.

PART IV

Modern Artificial Intelligence

CHAPTER 15

Can a Machine Think?

Overview

The question, "Can a machine think?" is one that has been debated for some time now and the question is no likely to be answered in this book. However, the subject is fruitful when considering "what a computer can do."

There are various opinions on the subject. Some say that thinking is an activity that is peculiar to human beings. Accordingly, machines cannot think. Although thought as something unique to humans may have been in the minds of early philosophers when they first considered the subject of thinking and intelligence, this does not really define the activity. Others maintain that a machine is thinking when it is performing activities that normally require thought when performed by human beings. Thus, adding 2+3 must be a form of thinking. To continue, some psychologists have defined intelligence in the following simple way: intelligence is what an intelligence test measures. In light of the preceding section on information systems, all that needs to be done is to feed enough information into an information system and to develop an appropriate query language, and the result is an intelligent machine. This line of reasoning also

skirts a clear definition. Perhaps, it is a waste of time to worry about precise definitions, but the fact remains that computers are doing some amazing things - such as playing chess, guiding robots, controlling space vehicles, recognizing patterns, proving theorems, and answering questions - and that these applications require much more than the conventional computer program. Richard Hamming, developer of the prestigious Hamming code for error detection and correction in computers, gives a definition of intelligent behavior that may be useful here:

> *The ability to act in subtle ways when presented with a class of situations that have not been exhaustively analyzed in advance, but which require rather different combinations of responses if the result in many specific cases is to be acceptable.*

Artificial Intelligence is an important subject because it may indicate the direction in which society is moving. Currently, machines are used for two reasons: (1) The job cannot be done by a human being, and (2) The job can be performed more economically by a machine. To this list, another reason must be added: some jobs are simply too dull to bed one by humans, and it is desirable from a social point of view to have such jobs done by machine. This requires a greater number of "intelligent" machines, since people seem to be finding more and more work they consider to be dull and routine.

Here are two items of before we get started with the talk:

Artificial general intelligence (AGI) is the intelligence of a machine that could successfully perform any intellectual task that a human being can. It is a primary goal of some AI research and is a common topic in science fiction and future studies. (Author unknown.)

The term singularity is used as the hypothesis that the invention of artificial super intelligence (ASI) will abruptly trigger runaway technical growth, resulting in unfathomable change to human civilization. (Author unknown)

It is possible to approach Artificial Intelligence from two points of view. Both approaches make use of programs and programming techniques. The first approach is to investigate the general principles of intelligence. The second is to study human thought, in particular.

Those persons engaged in the investigation of the principles of intelligence are normally charged with the development of systems that appear to be intelligent. This activity is commonly regarded as artificial Intelligence, which incorporates both engineering and computer science components.

Those persons engaged in the study of human thought attempt to emulate human mental processes to a lesser or greater

degree. This activity can be regarded as a form of "computer simulation," such that the elements of a relevant psychological theory are represented in a computer program. The objective of this approach is to generate psychological theories of human thought. The discipline is generally known as "Cognitive Science."

In reality, the differences between artificial intelligence and cognitive science tend to vary between "not so much" and "quite a lot" - depending upon the complexity of the underlying task. Most applications, as a matter of fact, contain elements from both approaches.

The Scope of AI

It is possible to zoom in on the scope of AI by focusing on the processes involved. At one extreme, the concentration is on the practicalities of doing AI programming, with an emphasis on symbolic programming languages and AI machines. In this context, AI can be regarded as a new way of doing programming. It necessarily follows that hardware/software systems with AI components have the potential for enhanced end-user effectiveness.

At the other extreme, AI could be regarded as the study of intelligent computation. This is a more grandiose and encompassing focus with the objective of building a systematic and encompassing focus with the objective of building a systematic theory of intellectual processes - regardless of if they model human thought or not.

It would appear, therefore, that AI is more concerned with intelligence in general and less involved with human thought in particular. Thus, it may be contended that humans and computers are simply two options in the genus of information processing systems.

The Modern Era of Artificial Intelligence

The modern era of artificial intelligence effectively began with the summer conference at Dartmouth College in Hanover, New Hampshire in 1956. The key participants were Shannon from Bell Labs, Minsky from Harvard (later M.I.T.), McCarthy from Dartmouth (later M.I.T. and Stanford), and Simon from Carnegie Tech (renamed Carnegie Mellon). The key results from the conference were twofold:

- It legitimized the notion of AI and brought together a raft of piecemeal research activities.
- The words Artificial Intelligence was coined and the name more than anything had a profound influence of the future direction of artificial intelligence.

The stars of the conference were Simon, and his associate Allen Newell, who demonstrated the Logic Theorist - the first well-known reasoning program. They preferred the name, "Complex Information Processing," for the new fledging science of the artificial. In the end, Shannon and McCarthy won out with the zippy and provocative name of artificial intelligence. In all probability, the resulting controversy surrounding the name

artificial intelligence served to sustain a certain critical mass of academic interest in the subject - even during periods of sporadic activity and questionable results.

One of the disadvantages of the pioneering AI conference was the simple fact that an elite group of scientists was created that would effectively decide "what AI is and what AI isn't," and how to best achieve it. The end result was that AI became closely aligned with psychology and not with neurophysiology and to a lesser degree with electrical engineering. AI became a software science with the main objective of producing intelligent artifacts. In short, it became a closed group, and this effectively constrained the field for a large degree. In a sense, that is the way the field exists today.

In recent years, the direction of AI research has been altered somewhat by an apparent relationship with brain research and cognitive technology, which is known as the design of joint human-machine cognitive systems. Two obvious fallouts of the new direction are the well-known "Connection Machine," and the computer vision projects at the National Bureau of Standards in their United States. That information is somewhat out of date, but the history gives some insight into what AI is today and where it will be heading.

Early Work on the Concept of Artificial Intelligence

The history of AI essentially goes back to the philosophy of Plato, who wrote that. "All knowledge must be state able in explicit definitions which anyone could apply," thereby eliminating appeals to judgment and intuition. Plato's student Aristotle continued in this noble tradition in the development of the categorical syllogism, which plays an important part in modern logic.

The mathematician Leibnitz attempted to quantify all knowledge and reasoning through an exact algebraic system by which all objects are assigned a unique characteristic number. Using these characteristic numbers, therefore, rules for the combination of problems would be established and controversies could be resolved by calculation.

The underlying philosophical idea was conceptually simple: Reduce the whole of human knowledge into a single formal system. The notion of formal representation has become the basis of AI and cognitive science theories since it involves the reduction of the totality of human experience to a set of basic elements that can be glued together in various ways.

To sum up, the philosophical phenomenologists argue that it impossible to subject pure phenomena - i.e., mental acts which give meaning to the world - to formal analysis. Of course, AI people do not agree. They contend that "there is no ghost in the

machine," and this is meant to imply that intelligence is a set of well-defined physical processes.

The discussion is reminiscent of the mind/brain controversy and it appears that the AI perspective is that "the mind is what the brain does." Of course, the phenomenologists would reply that the definition of mind exists beyond the physical neurons; it also incorporates the intangible concepts of what the neurons do.

Accordingly, strong AI is defined in the literature as the case wherein an appropriately programmed computer actually is a "mind." Weak AI, on the other hand, is the emulation of human intelligence, as we know it.

Cognitive Technology

Cognitive technology is the set of concepts and techniques for developing joint human-machine cognitive systems. People are obviously interested in cognitive systems because they are goal directed and employ self-knowledge of the environment to monitor, plan, and modify their actions in the pursuit of their goals. In a logical sense, joint human-machine systems can also be classed as being cognitive because of the availability of computational techniques for automating decisions and exercising operational control over physical processes and organizational activities.

Recent advances in heuristic techniques coupled with methods of knowledge representation and automated reasoning

have made it possible to couple human cognitive systems with artificial cognitive systems. Accordingly, joint systems in this case would necessarily have the following attributes:

- Be problem driven, rather than technology driven.
- Effective models of underlying processes are needed.
- Control of decision-making processes must be shared between human and artificial
- Clearly, cognitive technology represents a possible (if not probable) paradigm shift whereby the human self-view can and wake in the not-too-distant future.

Virtual Systems and Imagination

Methods for reasoning in expert and cognitive systems are well defined. Rules and representation effectively solve the problem. There appears to be a set of problems, however, that seem to evade such a simple solution as rules and representation.

A sophisticated model of a cognitive system must incorporate the capability of reasoning about itself or another cognitive system and about the computational facilities that provide the cognition. When a person, for example, is asked to reason about the feelings of the probable response of another person, set of rules is normally invoked to provide the desired response. If no rule set exists, then a virtual process is engaged that proceeds somewhat as follows:

- The object process is imagined.

- The neural inputs are "faked" and the brain responds in the usual manner.
- The result is observed exactly as though it had taken place.

Thus, a sort of simulation of a self-model is employed. This type of analysis might be invoked if someone were asked, for example, how they would feel if they had just received the news they had contracted an incurable disease.

The process, described above, is essentially what an operating system does while controlling the execution of a *guest* operating system. Inputs and outputs are interpreted, but machine code is actually executed.

It necessarily follows those executable models, as suggested here, are as much a form of knowledge as are rules and facts.

But, Is It intelligent?

Bandying the issue even further, a sharp borderline between intelligent and non-intelligent behavior, in the abstract sense, probably does not exist. Nevertheless, some essential qualities might be the following:

- To respond to situations very flexibly.
- To take advantage of fortuitous circumstances.
- To make sense out of ambiguous or contradictory input.
- To recognize the relative importance of different elements of a situation.

- To find similarities between situations despite differences which may separate them.
- To draw distinctions between situations despite similarities which may link them.
- To synthesize new concepts by taking old concepts And putting three together in new ways.
- To come up with ideas that they are novel.

Viewed in this manner, intelligence is a form of computation. Effective intelligence then is a process (perhaps a computer program) and an appropriate machine in which to execute the process.

Systems Concepts and AI

An interesting viewpoint concerns the evolution of data processing has emerged from the AI business. The task of designing a rule base and an associate fact base is somewhat analogous to designing an information system. Moreover, both kinds of systems appear to evolve in a similar manner. For this analysis, it should be assumed that statements and computational processes (i.e., modules) are the same (or synonymous).

A sensory stimulation is associated with a statement. (Incidentally, this concept is known as associations, wherein a sensation is associated with an idea, and that idea leads to another idea, and so forth. This theory originated with Aristotle and was pursued by Hobbs, Locke, and Mill.). The associations reverberate through the system of statements, whereby a result is finally

achieved. The output can be viewed as a prediction. Moreover, the system operates according to some form of internal laws - such as the laws of mathematics.

When a prediction fails, continuing with the statement analogy, we question the validity of the set of statements. Revisions are normally in order. Since a direct correlation is usually possible between the stimuli and peripheral statements, these statements are preserved from revision. Other statements must bear the brunt of change. The other statements, however, can be regarded as a Starting Point, since they result from internal laws. The end result that a priority judgment. Is necessary: change the peripheral statements of change the frozen middle. The priorities of course are in conflict and the preference commonly goes to the revision that disturbs the system the least.

Effectively, incremental changes are made to the system until a total revision is necessary - i.e., a rewrite of the internal including the Laws, the frozen middle, and the peripheral statements. As a total concept, major revisions serve to simplify a system. It necessarily follows that some attention should be given to systems evolution as a predictive technique.

CHAPTER 16

Thinking

An academic named John Dewey specialized in thinking, at least for a while anyway, and wrote the popular book entitled *How We Think* that was translated into several languages. At first, the emphasis of thinking was to solve problems and consisted of the scientific method, reflective thinking, and the role of the educator in public life; it consisted of reading, writing, and arithmetic and subsequently the academic subjects of history, mathematics, and chemistry. Dewey's work was organized around some aspect of educational learning, associated with the Laboratory School at the University of Chicago. Dewey defined reflective thought as the active, persistent, and appropriate examination of beliefs of the information that is available. Thoughts are a continuum of several beliefs. Dewey says that the scientific method of behavior involves deferring to make judgment until sufficient data is obtained and testing, or verification, is done. Dewey has developed five steps, relevant to AI, that constitute reflective thought. (1) Development of the uncertainty requiring the reflective thought. (2) Defining the problem to be solved. (3) Collection of data and other factors relevant to the problem. (4) Construction of suitable hypotheses. (5) Development of methods to solve the problem.

One of the leading persons in developing conceptual ideas about intelligent computers was an English scientist name Alan Turing, the mathematician that broke the German cryptographic code that helped the U.S., Great Britain, and other countries - called the Allies - win World War II," continued Matt. Alan Turing was a forward looking individual and was involved with several academic pursuits. One of the most popular was the *Turing Test* for determining whether a computer and its program were intelligent or not. On the surface, it seems pretty simple minded, but it gave people something to think about; I am supposed to be looking into thinking. He proposed that if a person gave a question to a person and a computer, and could not tell if the written answer was from the computer or a person then we could say that the computer was thinking, that is exhibiting intelligence, that is artificial intelligence. It seems to be a little simple minded, but it makes some sense. Of course, there is no mention of how the computer would do it

Relevant concepts on thinking that would serve as an aid to someone desiring to learn something about thinking.

1. Every involving thought has to go through the mind, person or computer.
2. Everything we say goes through our heads.
3. Thinking usually involves matters not directly perceived.
4. Thought involves belief in something accepted or believed.
5. Thoughts implied by certain beliefs are the source of additional beliefs.

6. Thoughts caused by events remind a person of related consequences.
7. Curiosities that cause senses are achieved through thinking.

Why is thinking of concern to the development of AI systems? That is because AI thinking precludes AI behavior.

CHAPTER 17

Learning

———— ⚬⚬⚬ ————

The term *learning* in an Artificial Intelligence context is the form of activity that results in purposeful behavior. In short, the AI software learns what to do to solve a problem in very much the same way it is done in the minds of humans. In AI systems, the AI software and human thinking work together to resolve a specific class of problems."

In AI, what is learned? Is it the method, the solution, or both.

Machine intelligence and learning reflects a computer system that exhibits behavior that would be classified as intelligent if performed by a human agent. That computer system would be known as an intelligent agent, and that field of study is termed *artificial intelligence.* Some researchers refer to AI, as it is usually called, as that which hasn't been done yet, even though that term doesn't seem to make sense in today's computer world. That would imply that an intelligent agent should, in fact, perform a certain amount of learning.

Some researchers feel as though AI can be achieved when human intelligence can be described in sufficient detail that a machine can be made to simulate it. One of the early artificial

intelligent applications is computer chess, wherein the program emulates a human chess player. Some AI applications can learn how to play a game and win by learning how to operate without human intervention.

In general, AI researchers feel that any problem that can be solved by a human can be developed as an AI application, and the challenger is to have the AI program learn by itself how to play. That is why machine learning is one of the most important concepts in artificial intelligence.

Other disciplines can be related to machine intelligence, such as advanced statistical techniques, which is termed *deep learning*. There are several topics related to machine intelligence and learning:

- Reasoning and problem solving
- Knowledge representation
- Knowledge engineering
- Qualification
- Natural language
- Creativity
- General intelligence

AI is relevant to any task that can demonstrate intelligence. As before, when a term (or technique) reaches mainstream, it is no longer considered artificial intelligence. This is the *AI effect*. Here

are some worthy applications: Healthcare, Automotive, Finance, and Video Games. There are two basic questions:

- Is artificial general intelligence possible? Can a machine solve any problem that a human can solve?
- Are intelligent machines dangerous?"

Machine learning is a complicated subject in artificial intelligence.

END OF CHAPTER SEVENTEEN

CHAPTER 18

The Advisor Model

―――――――――― ∾ ――――――――――

An expert-system is characterized by a database of facts and a logical engine for exploiting the facts in a purposeful manner. The logical engine takes good advantage of the available information so that the output of the system is considerably more than what would ordinarily be implied strictly by the input. The data and the inference programs give the system an air of being an expert.

One of the most illustrative examples of an expert system is the well-known wine advisor. The user enters a brief description of an entrée, such as chicken with cream sauce, and the system yields a small wine selection, such as Chardonnay or Montrachet – depending of course upon the current contents of the wine cellar. Naturally, there is more to the story. The entrée has certain characteristics that are determined by a database search. The characteristics are then used by an inference mechanism during a "run" of the system to generate the attributes of a suitable wine, such as color, taste, and strength (i.e., light, heavy, etc.) In a second database operation, the wine attributes are mapped into a "variety" of wine. Finally, a selection is made from the database that represents the contents of the wine cellar.

Similar advisors have been constructed in the financial community and in the nuclear industry – to name only a few.

In an investment advisor, for example, an investor's profile is mapped into a well-defined, but much larger, set of investment characteristics using a database operation. Again, an inference mechanism is used; in this case, it generates a portfolio structure that serves as input to a database search operation yielding a set of investment options. A typical portfolio structure might be: 60% equities, 35% bonds, and 5% gold. The output set would be a small selection of instruments in selected currencies.

In the nuclear industry, a collection of physical events occurring in an emergency situation would be translated by an expert system into a set of instructions to an operator. As before, the processing sequence includes an initial database search operation, an inference procedure, and then a final database selection to generate the needed instructions. The examples typify the "advisor model."

The *advisor model* is characterized by the following set of actions occurring in essentially the order given:

- A relatively small set of input values are entered into the system via and end user interaction or as the result of a physical event.
- The input values are expanded into the particulars for a certain problem domain via a database search process.
- The particulars are mapped into a set of descriptors via an inference mechanism that can take the form of a set of if-then rules and a logical engine, a neural network, a

pattern matching operation, a mathematical function, or possibly logic program.

- The descriptors are used as key values in a subsequent database search operation to yield the results for that problem.

Clearly, the salient properties of the advisor model are the initial database operation, the inference (or mapping) process, and the final database search. The two database operations are obviously to different structures. Each of these components can be replicated, as required by a particular problem and its problem solver, but the general structure of the model is evident without necessarily going into more detail. In fact, most expert systems operate in precisely this manner, even though the emphasis has conventionally been on the rules and knowledge-based parts of the model.

The advisor model is independent of the mode of representation; this fact is tacitly understood and is inherent in the notion of a model. Representation is dependent upon a specific instantiation of the model. If the cells in a spreadsheet application are the source of information, then the retrieval and inference operations are related to that framework. If the inference processes are implemented as LISP or Prolog programs, then the particulars and descriptors are constrained by the corresponding ad hoc data structures. To sum up, the method of representation is determined by the underlying problem domain and computational framework. This explains to a limited degree why a lot more "advisors" are not floating around in the industrial, academic, and governmental

communities. The ultimate objective is clear: to make the benefits of the advisor model available in a general-purpose format.

Another consideration that complicates the picture is the existence of uncertainty in most areas dealings with human affairs. Uncertainty has been the Achilles heel of the artificial intelligence community, since a practical system for problem solving should take the uncertainty of information or the uncertainty of the reasoning process into consideration. Naturally, we would like to have the mechanisms in place for dealing effectively with both forms of uncertainty, even though all of the features may not be needed for a particular problem situation. It is indeed one thing to map an entrée of beef into a wine descriptor in a deterministic sense, such as:

beef -> strong red meat -> dry heavy red wine -> …

and quite another to introduce the notion of uncertainty, as in:

small lump -> (((healthy, tests))),0.6),((healthy, tests, sick),0.4))

->… -> ((home, office).0.56)

The notation in the latter example is intended to demonstrate that a *small lump* is mapped into the conditions of *healthy* or *tests* with a certainty of 0.6 and into the conditions of *healthy* or *tests* or *sick* with a certainty factor of 0.4. Total comprehension here

is not expected, but is given to indicate that there are different ways to use AI.

In the wine and medical examples, there is relatively little complication in the advisory process, and gives us the opportunity of focusing on the initial database operation. The process represents a translation between the external world of the end user to the internal world of the automated problem solver In the wine advisor, for example, the indicator of beef is mapped into a set of attributes with which AI model can work, as in:

beef -> strong red meat

or in its generic form:

indicator -> meaning

The notion of an indicator is well-established in organized society in the form of symbols, variables, synonyms, and abbreviations. It is commonplace to have an indicator, such as *successful,* that is associated with a substantial set of characteristics, such as *aggressive, confident, intelligent, and focused.* Indicators can have different meanings to different people' however, which preserves the role of the expert. In the absence of uncertainly, and indicator has a definite meaning. In the presence of uncertainty, an indicator *might* mean something, and the degree to which an expert believes the assertion is known as its certainty value, or as its the certainty factor, as it is sometimes called. Thus, the

indicator in the presence of uncertainty is a clue to the validity of an assertion; it becomes evidence when combined with its meaning and a certainty value, or in its generic form:

Evidence: *indicator -> meaning with certainly value.*

An obvious consideration applies to the notion of evidence. As in common everyday usage, a fact "is entered as evidence" only when it is relevant to the case under consideration. An analogous caveat applies to the methods contained here, and a means is presented for constraining the relevancy of information.

CHAPTER 19

Conversational Programs

———————————————————ᨆ———————————————————

Alan Turing is an English mathematician whose work on cryptography was a major contribution to the victory in World War II. Almost single handedly, he developed a machine that could solve the German's cryptographic enigma code that was used to win the war for the allies. He is also very well known for the development of basic concepts in mathematics and computation. Alan Turing received his PhD from Princeton University.

Dr. Turing is best known for a variety of intellectual concepts, but the most well-known is the Turing Test for artificial intelligence. The fundamental idea is based on the idea that a computer exhibits intelligence when it can answer questions, and a person can or cannot tell that it is a computer answering the questions. The basic result is that if a computer is mistaken for a human more than 30% of time during a set of keyboard interactions, then it is exhibiting intelligence. The test works as follows. There are three computers connected together and two people and one supposedly intelligent program. One person asks the questions and the other two computers answer the question. If the program can answer the questions and it is undetectable that is a the computer, then that program exhibits intelligence. Turing

also gives conditions for conducting the "Turing test," but that is the basic idea behind the test.

There is another AI-type program named ELIZA developed by Joseph Weizenbaum at MIT in 1966. The on-line program uses the input to determine the response, as in non-directive counseling in Psychology. ELIZA is on-line and here is no secret about how it operates. Yet, so many people begin to believe it, that many universities - including MIT - had to take it offline.

The user person just says things to ELIZA and ELIZA responds just like an ordinary person would, using the information in the person's input. The ELIZA program is not that simple. It has to stay on the beam, so to speak. Most people don't think of that when they think of Artificial Intelligence, but it would seem to have intelligence.

There is an Experimental Scientist from Hungary that has looked into the subject of conversational programs and has written a book on the subject. I'll give the reference later. The program, ELIZA, contains a collection of patterns and a collection of answers corresponding to the patterns. There is another program, like DOCTOR. There is a third system named PARRY. It is interesting when they put DOCTOR and PARRY together. The PARRY program also is known to deceive practicing psychiatrists.

The reference is: Mérö, László, *Ways of Thinking: The Limits of Rational Thought and Artificial Intelligence,* New Jersey: World Scientific Publishing Co., 1990. There is a movie on Alan Turing titled *The Imitation Game.*

CHAPTER 20

How We Think

———— ⁓ ————

There is not a lot of literature on precisely what thinking is. An academic named John Dewey specialized in it, at least for a while anyway, and wrote the popular book entitled How We Think. At first, the emphasis of thinking was to solve problems and consisted of the scientific method, reflective thinking, and the role of the educator in public life; it consisted of reading, writing, and arithmetic and subsequently the academic subjects of history, mathematics, and chemistry. Dewey defined reflective thought as the active, persistent, and appropriate examination of beliefs of the information that is available. Thoughts are a continuum of several beliefs. Dewey says that the scientific method of behavior involves deferring to make judgment until sufficient data is obtained and testing, or verification, is done. Dewey has developed five steps, relevant to AI, that constitute reflective thought. (1) Development of the uncertainty requiring the reflective thought. (2) Defining the problem to be solved. (3) Collection of data and other factors relevant to the problem. (4) Construction of suitable hypotheses. (5) Development of methods to solve the problem.

The term learning in an Artificial Intelligence context is the form of activity that results in purposeful behavior. In short, the AI software learns what to do to solve a problem in very much

the same way it is done in the minds of humans. In AI systems, the AI software and human thinking work together to resolve a specific class of problems. In AI, what is learned? Is it the method, solution, or both.

At this point, it seems like nothing is learned. Some smart person designs a problem and writes a computer program to solve the problem, and it is called Artificial Intelligence and it supposed to be intelligent. That's the problem with this problem, information is scattered all over the place and who knows what it means. Here is a example of the current situation, as a whole. "Go to a well-known retail store that sells just about everything including food and computers, looking for a cartridge for your printer, and there is a kid working there who says 'we have computers and artificial intelligence'. He really should have said software, but how was he to know what artificial intelligence is unless there is some reliable place where he should go for information. You can see what you are up against. We are finished with thinking and are looking for some small applications to use as examples.

A Quick Look at ChatGPT

ChatGPT is called a form of *Generative AI*, like everyone reading about it knows what Generative AI is. Here is a list all of those new made-up names. At least the ones that are easy to run across. In a system of this type, there seem to be three entities: a foundation of information in various forms, an application model that accesses the data, that can be any form imaginable, and a sophisticated front that generates the information in the form the user requests it. All three entities are complicated. In my mind, ChatGPT is a system that generates information for the end user. It is analogous to the big computer, years ago called a mainframe, that initially performed a task for the end user."

Here is a list of ChatGPT definitions:

Chat GPT stands for Generative Pre-trained Transform.

Chat GPT is analogous to the results produced on customer service websites - ask questions and get answers.

ChatGPT is an AI program called a chatbot that employs natural language processing to create a humanlike conversational dialogue.

The language model responds to questions and can create various forms of written context, such as articles, messages, emails, computer programs, and media posts. Maybe even artwork.

The natural language processing includes machine translation, information retrieval, sentence analysis, and information extraction.

ChatGPT is a kind of generative AI that involves entering prompts and receiving humanlike images, test, or video.

ChatGPT is similar it automated results and services that are found on customer service websites: ask questions and receive clarification.

ChatGPT is trained with reinforcement learning through human feedback and reward systems that analyze and rank the responses. This is machine learning.

ChatGPT is a product of ca company named OpenAI.

ChatGPT uses algorithms to find patterns within data sequences.

ChatGPT uses deep learning to produce text with the use of neural networks.

ChatPT produces text, next word, sentences, or paragraphs based on some learning formulation.

Human trainers provide conversations to test and rank results.

ChartGPT has been used to code computer programs, compose music, writ emails, summarize articles, write social memos, make titles, solve math problems s, create articles, reword existing content, make product descriptions, play games, do job searches, and ask questions like in ELIZA.

ChatGPT has limitations does have limitations, such as the complexity of human language, use up to date data, poor on analytics, doesn't get the subtleties of modern language, and has trouble focusing on what data is relevant to a problem.

ChatGPT has some ethics problems such as privacy, security, cheating in education, and cheating at work.

ChatGPT has problems of plagiarism, bias, fireplaces, human jibs, and cost.

Someone has said that ChatGPT is a good place to start learning what artificial intelligence is all about.

A Very Quick Summary of Modern AI

In the next couple of chapters and the final report, here is a quick summary of what you are going to have to know to understand what is going on in the AI world:

Machine Learning

Machine learning is area of study in Artificial Intelligence that is. Usually divided into two categories: Supervisor learning and Unsupervised learning. It is usually considered when designing large scale AI systems. It is normally referred to as an enabler.

Cognitive Computing

Cognitive computing is a technique to develop computers that behave like the human mind through the AI techniques such as expert systems, neural networks, and machine learning. This statement has been tagged for a rewrite.

Types of AI

Types of AI includes most concepts that exist within the AI domain, such as: weak AI, strong AI, deep learning, machine

learning, reactive machines, spatial computing, generative AI, facial recognition, chat bots, synthetic data, contrastive learning, and so on. The is a complex section.

Watson System

Watson is an IBM system that provides a conversational AI system that can service in a large variety of disciplines. It typically is integrated into a larger system as services as an interactive assisted designed to handle large databases and other information domains. Practically every element of existing AI technology is provided with Watson.

Machine Learning

—⁓—

Artificial Intelligence Specifics

It is the study and development of techniques for making machines that people would class as being smart, especially computer systems and programs. It involves the study of human intelligence, but it is not limited to what we would class as human activity. Thus, the subject of Artificial Intelligence defines the concept of intelligence for its own purpose. Like saying a checkers program is intelligent.

At this point in its development, there are no systems that are more intelligent than humans. There are programs that do very complicated things, however, and they are under the control of other computers or human beings.

The goals of Artificial Intelligence are the development of machines - usually computers - that can think and act like human beings and incorporate thinking and acting accordingly.

Theoretically, the scope of Artificial Intelligence ranges from simple programs to systems that are more intelligent than humans. Many people believe that Artificial Intelligent machines

will take over the civilized world, and just as many, perhaps more, think that is not true.

Machine Learning Specifics

There are two types of Artificial Intelligence: weak AI and strong AI. *Weak AI is* sometimes referred to as *Narrow AI,* since people like fancy names and also *Artificial Narrow Intelligence* (ANI), that are designed to perform specific small tasks. Some ANI systems are exceedingly simple like vacuum cleaners that can roan around the living room, and a little more complicated self-driving cars and IBM's Watson.

Strong AI is a group of AI's, including Artificial General Intelligence (AGI) or Artificial Super Intelligent (ASI) with intelligence equal to humans. It could do anything, such as solve problems and plan for the future. It would have super intelligence. Strong idea is a good idea, to some degree, but doesn't exist today.

This opens the door to deep learning and machine learning. Since the two names are used interchangeably, it is prudent to denote the difference between them. Machine learning is a sub area of Artificial Intelligence, and deep learning is a sub area of machine learning.

The types of learning differ in how the algorithm learns. Non-deep learning uses human experts to analyze data while deep learning does it by itself.

Deep learning employs neural networks and is generally considered mor of what Artificial Intelligence should be. Neural networks is with Quantum Computing as two of the most complicated subject in advance computer technology.

Generative models take raw data and generate useful information. Generative models take raw data and generate useful information. Generate models are not new and are what the subject of statistics is designed to do. The modern Artificial Intelligence method use information to select data for display or other forms of computation.

Artificial Intelligence Applications

Most Artificial Intelligence writers summarize into 5 categories. They are: Speech Recognition, Customer Service, Computer Vision, Recommendation Engines, and Automated Stock Trading. Here is a brief summary of those categories.

Speech: Uses natural language processing to analyze human speech and generate it in a written form.

Customer: Called virtual agents that respond to customer queries, that may be questions, products, and sizes through customer engagement. Referred to as virtual agents or voice assistants.

<u>Vision:</u> Used to derive useful information from digital images and videos. Used in healthcare, law enforcement, or design by computer.

<u>Recommendation:</u> Use past consumption to discover data trends to improve various business goals.

<u>Automated:</u> Used to optimize stock portfolios and facilitate automated stock trading.

There you have it.

Cognitive Computing

—⁓—

The fundamental stating point of modern AI is the nebulous subject generally known as cognitive computing. Here is a list of cognitive subjects:

> Conventional computing and cognitive computing
> Machine conversation
> Compute vision
> Computer speaking
> Empathy from computers
> Discovery and understanding of unstructured content (Watson subject)
> Cognitive systems (Watson subject)

On the surface the list is subject are straight forward subject, but they are exceedingly complicated.

Conventional computing and cognitive computing

Convention computing is, as practically everyone knows, is a pre-planned set of steps to provide a per-planned result. With convention, applications are conceived, designed, programmed or coded, tested, and then put into operation through a person-oriented scenario. The only intelligence is in the mind of the

person's involved. The objectives are identified beforehand, and additionally, computing elements are designed to interact of a pre-defined manner.

With cognitive computing, elements are defined and combined to execute in an intelligent manner without human intervention. The computing elements may be defined and prepared or exist in the outside operational environment.

Machine Conversation

Machine conversation is a defined collection of natural language processing and machine learning elements. In its most simple form it is two conversational programs that talk to one another, such as ELIZA and ELIZA or DOCTOR and DOCTOR, mentioned previously in this report. Intelligent machine conversation involves two compatible intelligent entities interactions with one another.

Computer Speaking

The ability to initiate computer speech is a companion to speech recognition. It is usually combined with speech recognition and cognitive computing. A simple example is text reading and speaking. When combined with other cognitive elements, it is in the AI domain.

Empathy from Computers

There are two kinds of computer empathy: human empathy for computer technology and its various difficulties, and the empathy of computers to humans. Computer can sense emotion if defined beforehand. As yet, it has not been considered in the area of Artificial Intelligence.

Cognitive Systems

The discovery and understanding of unstructured information and cognitive sysems is generally combined under the title Generative Models.

A generative model is a deep learning facility that can take raw data, such as database information, speech, visual information, and other event data and draw relevant conclusions.

Modern Artificial Intelligence Summary

—⁓—

(Duplications included for continuity)

The question, "Can a machine think?" is one that has been debated for some time now and the question is no likely to be answered in this book. However, the subject is fruitful when considering "what a computer can do."

Overview

There are various opinions on the subject. Some say that thinking is an activity that is peculiar to human beings. Accordingly, machines cannot think. Although thought as something unique to humans may have been in the minds of early philosophers when they first considered the subject of thinking and intelligence, this does not really define the activity. Others maintain that a machine is thinking when it is performing activities that normally require thought when performed by human beings. Thus, adding 2+3 must be a form of thinking. To continue, some psychologists have defined intelligence in the following simple way: intelligence is what an intelligence test measures. In light of the preceding section on information systems, all that needs

to be done is to feed enough information into an information system and to develop an appropriate query language, and the result is an intelligent machine. This line of reasoning also skirts a clear definition. Perhaps, it is a waste of time to worry about precise definitions, but the fact remains that computers are doing some amazing things - such as playing chess, guiding robots, controlling space vehicles, recognizing patterns, proving theorems, and answering questions - and that these applications require much more than the conventional computer program. Richard Hamming, developer of the prestigious Hamming code for error detection and correction in computers, gives a definition of intelligent behavior that may be useful here:

> *The ability to act in subtle ways when presented with a class of situations that have not been exhaustively analyzed in advance, but which require rather different combinations of responses if the result in many specific cases is to be acceptable.*

Artificial Intelligence is an important subject because it may indicate the direction in which society is moving. Currently, machines are used for two reasons: (1) The job cannot be done by a human being, and (2) The job can be performed more economically by a machine. To this list, another reason must be added: some jobs are simply too dull to bed one by humans, and it is desirable from a social point of view to have such jobs done by machine. This requires a greater number of "intelligent" machines, since people seem to be finding more and more work they consider to be dull and routine.

Here are two items of before we get started with the talk:

> *Artificial general intelligence (AGI) is the intelligence of a machine that could successfully perform any intellectual task that a human being can. It is a primary goal of some AI research and is a common topic in science fiction and future studies. (Author unknown.)*

> *The term singularity is used as the hypothesis that the invention of artificial super intelligence (ASI) will abruptly trigger runaway technical growth, resulting in unfathomable change to human civilization. (Author unknown)*

It is possible to approach Artificial Intelligence from two points of view. Both approaches make use of programs and programming techniques. The first approach is to investigate the general principles of intelligence. The second is to study human thought, in particular.

Those persons engaged in the investigation of the principles of intelligence are normally charged with the development of systems that appear to be intelligent. This activity is commonly regarded as "artificial intelligence," which incorporates both engineering and computer science components.

Those persons engaged in the study of human thought attempt to emulate human mental processes to a lesser or greater

degree. This activity can be regarded as a form of "computer simulation," such that the elements of a relevant psychological theory are represented in a computer program. The objective of this approach is to generate psychological theories of human thought. The discipline is generally known as "Cognitive Science."

In reality, the differences between artificial intelligence and cognitive science tend to vary between "not so much" and "quite a lot" - depending upon the complexity of the underlying task. Most applications, as a matter of fact, contain elements from both approaches.

The Scope of AI

It is possible to zoom in on the scope of AI by focusing on the processes involved. At one extreme, the concentration is on the practicalities of doing AI programming, with an emphasis on symbolic programming languages and AI machines. In this context, AI can be regarded as a new way of doing programming. It necessarily follows that hardware/software systems with AI components have the potential for enhanced end-user effectiveness.

At the other extreme, AI could be regarded as the study of intelligent computation. This is a more grandiose and encompassing focus with the objective of building a systematic and encompassing focus with the objective of building a systematic theory of intellectual processes - regardless of if they model human thought or not.

It would appear, therefore, that AI is more concerned with intelligence in general and less involved with human thought in particular. Thus, it may be contended that humans and computers are simply two options in the genus of information processing systems.

The Modern Era of Artificial Intelligence

The modern era of artificial intelligence effectively began with the summer conference at Dartmouth College in Hanover, New Hampshire in 1956. The key participants were Shannon from Bell Labs, Minsky from Harvard (later M.I.T.), McCarthy from Dartmouth (later M.I.T. and Stanford), and Simon from Carnegie Tech (renamed Carnegie Mellon). The key results from the conference were twofold:

> *It legitimized the notion of AI and brought together a raft of piecemeal research activities.*

> *The name Artificial Intelligence was coined and the name more than anything had a profound influence of the future direction of artificial intelligence.*

The stars of the conference were Simon, and his associate Allen Newell, who demonstrated the Logic Theorist - the first well-known reasoning program. They preferred the name, "Complex Information Processing," for the new fledging science of the artificial. In the end, Shannon and McCarthy won out

with the zippy and provocative name, "artificial intelligence." In all probability, the resulting controversy surrounding the name artificial intelligence served to sustain a certain critical mass of academic interest in the subject - even during periods of sporadic activity and questionable results.

One of the disadvantages of the pioneering AI conference was the simple fact that an elite group of scientists was created that would effectively decide "what AI is and what AI isn't," and how to best achieve it. The end result was that AI became closely aligned with psychology and not with neurophysiology and to a lesser degree with electrical engineering. AI became a software science with the main objective of producing intelligent artifacts. In short, it became a closed group, and this effectively constrained the field for a large degree. In a sense, that is the way the field exists today.

In recent years, the direction of AI research has been altered somewhat by an apparent relationship with brain research and cognitive technology, which is known as the design of joint human-machine cognitive systems. Two obvious fallouts of the new direction are the well-known "Connection Machine," and the computer vision projects at the National Bureau of Standards in their United States. That information is somewhat out of date, but the history gives some insight into what AI is today and where it will be heading.

Early Work on the Concept of Artificial Intelligence

The history of AI essentially goes back to the philosophy of Plato, who wrote that. "All knowledge must be state able in explicit definitions which anyone could apply," thereby eliminating appeals to judgment and intuition. Plato's student Aristotle continued in this noble tradition in the development of the categorical syllogism, which plays an important part in modern logic.

The mathematician Leibnitz attempted to quantify all knowledge and reasoning through an exact algebraic system by which all objects are assigned a unique characteristic number. Using these characteristic numbers, therefore, rules for the combination of problems would be established and controversies could be resolved by calculation.

The underlying philosophical idea was conceptually simple: Reduce the whole of human knowledge into a single formal system. The notion of formal representation has become the basis of AI and cognitive science theories since it involves the reduction of the totality of human experience to a set of basic elements that can be glued together in various ways.

To sum up, the philosophical phenomenologists argue that it impossible to subject pure phenomena - i.e., mental acts which give meaning to the world - to formal analysis. Of course, AI people do not agree. They contend that "there is no ghost in the

machine," and this is meant to imply that intelligence is a set of well-defined physical processes.

The discussion is reminiscent of the mind/brain controversy and it appears that the AI perspective is that "the mind is what the brain does." Of course, the phenomenologists would reply that the definition of mind exists beyond the physical neurons; it also incorporates the intangible concepts of what the neurons do.

Accordingly, strong AI is defined in the literature as the case wherein an appropriately programmed computer actually is a "mind." Weak AI, on the other hand, is the emulation of human intelligence, as we know it.

Intelligence and Intelligent Systems

There seems to be some value in the ongoing debate over the intelligence of AI artifacts. The term "artificial" in artificial intelligence helps us out. One could therefore contend that intelligence is natural if it is biological and artificial otherwise. This conclusion skirts the controversy and frees intellectual energy for more purposeful activity.

The abstract notion of intelligence, therefore, is conceptualized, and natural and artificial intelligence serve as specific instances. The subjects of understanding and learning could be treated in a similar manner. The productive tasks of identifying the salient aspects of intelligence, understanding, and learning emerge as the combined goal of AI and cognitive science. For example,

the concepts of representation and reasoning, to name only two of many, have been studied productively from both artificial and biological viewpoints. Software products that are currently available can be evaluated in the basis of how well they can support the basic AI technologies,

The key question then becomes: How well do natural and artificial systems, as discussed above, match up to the abstract notion of intelligence.

Cognitive Technology

Cognitive technology is the set of concepts and techniques for developing joint human-machine cognitive systems. People are obviously interested in cognitive systems because they are goal directed and employ self-knowledge of the environment to monitor, plan, and modify their actions in the pursuit of their goals. In a logical sense, joint human-machine systems can also be classed as being cognitive because of the availability of computational techniques for automating decisions and exercising operational control over physical processes and organizational activities.

Recent advances in heuristic techniques coupled with methods of knowledge representation and automated reasoning have made it possible to couple human cognitive systems with artificial cognitive systems. Accordingly, joint systems in this case would necessarily have the following attributes:

- Be problem driven, rather than technology driven
- Effective models of underlying processes are needed.
- Control of decision-making processes must be shared between human and artificial components.

Clearly, cognitive technology represents a possible (if not probable) paradigm shift whereby the human self-view can and wake in the not-too-distant future.

Virtual Systems and Imagination

Methods for reasoning in expert and cognitive systems are well defined. Rules and representation effectively solve the problem. There appears to be a set of problems, however, that seem to evade such a simple solution as rules and representation.

A sophisticated model of a cognitive system must incorporate the capability of reasoning about itself or another cognitive system and about the computational facilities that provide the cognition. When a person, for example, is asked to reason about the feelings of the probable response of another person, set of rules is normally invoked to provide the desired response. If no rule set exists, then a virtual process is engaged that proceeds somewhat as follows:

- The object process is imagined.
- The neural inputs are "faked" and the brain responds in the usual manner.
- The result is observed exactly as though it had taken place.

Thus, a sort of simulation of a self-model is employed. This type of analysis might be invoked if someone were asked, for example, how they would feel if they had just received the news they had contracted an incurable disease.

The process, described above, is essentially what an operating system does while controlling the execution of a "guest" operating system. Inputs and outputs are interpreted, but machine code is actually executed.

It necessarily follows those executable models, as suggested here, are as much a form of knowledge as are rules and facts.

Is It intelligent?

Bandying the issue even further, a sharp borderline between intelligent and non-intelligent behavior, in the abstract sense, probably does not exist. Nevertheless, some essential qualities might be the following:

- To respond to situations very flexibly.
- To take advantage of fortuitous circumstances.
- To make sense out of ambiguous or contradictory messages.
- To recognize the relative importance of different elements of a situation.
- To find similarities between situations despite differences which may separate them.
- To draw distinctions between situations despite similarities which may link them.

- To synthesize new concepts by taking old concepts And putting three together in new ways.
- To come up with ideas that they are novel.

Viewed in this manner, intelligence is a form of computation. Effective intelligence then is a process (perhaps a computer program) and an appropriate machine in which to execute the process.

Systems Concepts and AI

An interesting viewpoint concerns the evolution of data processing has emerged from the AI business. The task of designing a rule base and an associate fact base is somewhat analogous to designing an information system. Moreover, both kinds of systems appear to evolve in a similar manner. For this analysis, it should be assumed that statements and computational processes (i.e., modules) are the same (or synonymous).

A sensory stimulation is associated with a statement. (Incidentally, this concept is known as associations, wherein a sensation is associated with an idea, and that idea leads to another idea, and so forth. This theory originated with Aristotle and was pursued by Hobbs, Locke, and Mill.). The associations reverberate through the system of statements, whereby a result is finally achieved. The output can be viewed as a prediction. Moreover, the system operates according to some form of internal laws - such as the laws of mathematics.

When a prediction fails, continuing with the statement analogy, we question the validity of the set of statements. Revisions are normally in order. Since a direct correlation is usually possible between the stimuli and peripheral statements, these statements are preserved from revision. Other statements must bear the brunt of change. The other statements, however, can be regarded as the "frozen middle," since they result from internal laws. The end result that a priority judgment. Is necessary: change the peripheral statements of change the frozen middle. The priorities of course are in conflict and the preference commonly goes to the revision that disturbs the system the least.

Effectively, incremental changes are made to the system until a total revision is necessary - i.e., a rewrite of the internal including the rules, the frozen middle, and the peripheral statements. As a total concept, major revisions serve to simplify a system. It necessarily follows that some attention should be given to systems evolution as a predictive technique.

Thinking

An academic named John Dewey specialized in it, at least for a while anyway, and wrote the popular book entitled How We Think. At first, the emphasis of thinking was to solve problems and consisted of the scientific method, reflective thinking, and the role of the educator in public life; it consisted of reading, writing, and arithmetic and subsequently the academic subjects of history, mathematics, and chemistry. Dewey defined reflective thought as the active, persistent, and appropriate examination of beliefs of the

information that is available. Thoughts are a continuum of several beliefs. Dewey says that the scientific method of behavior involves deferring to make judgment until sufficient data is obtained and testing, or verification, is done. Dewey has developed five steps, relevant to AI, that constitute reflective thought. (1) Development of the uncertainty requiring the reflective thought. (2) Defining the problem to be solved. (3) Collection of data and other factors relevant to the problem. (4) Construction of suitable hypotheses. (5) Development of methods to solve the problem.

The term <u>learning</u> in an Artificial Intelligence context is the form of activity that results in purposeful behavior. In short, the AI software learns what to do to solve a problem in very much the same way it is done in the minds of humans. In AI systems, the AI software and human thinking work together to resolve a specific class of problems. In AI, what is learned? Is it the method, solution, or both.

At this point, it seems like nothing is learned. Some smart person designs a problem and writes a computer program to solve the problem, and it is called Artificial Intelligence and it supposed to be intelligent. That's the problem with this problem, information is scattered all over the place and who knows what it means. I went to a well-known retail store that sells just about everything including food and computers. I was looking for a cartridge for our printer, and this kid working there says we have computers and artificial intelligence. He really should have said software, but how was he to know what artificial intelligence is unless there is some reliable place where he should go for

information. You can see what you are up against. We are finished with thinking and are looking for some small applications to use as examples.

A Quick Look at ChatGPT

Chat GPT stands for Generative Transform.

Chat GPT is analogous to the results produced on customer service websites - ask questions and get answers.

ChatGPT is an AI program called a chatbot that employs natural language processing to create a humanlike conversational dialogue.

The language model responds to questions and can create various forms of written context, such as articles, messages, emails, computer programs, and media posts. Maybe even artwork.

The natural language processing includes machine translation, information retrieval, sentence analysis, and information extraction.

ChatGPT is a kind of generative AI that involves entering prompts and receiving humanlike images, test, or video in return.

ChatGPT is similar it automated results and services that are found on customer service websites: ask questions and receive clarification.

Chat GPT is trained with reinforcement learning through human feedback and reward systems that analyze and rank the responses. This is machine learning.

ChatGPT is a product of a company named OpenAI.

ChatGPT uses algorithms to find patterns within data sequences.

ChatGPT uses deep learning to produce text with the use of neural networks.

ChatPT produces text, next word, sentences, or paragraphs based on some learning formulation.

Machine Learning and Types of AI

It is the study and development of techniques for making machines that people would class as being smart, especially computer systems and programs. It involves the study of human intelligence, but it is not limited to what we would class as human activity. Thus, the subject of Artificial Intelligence defines the concept of intelligence for its own purpose. Like saying a checkers program is intelligent.

At this point in its development, there are no systems that are more intelligent than humans. There are programs that do very complicated things, however, and they are under the control of other computers or human beings.

The goals of Artificial Intelligence are the development of machines - usually computers - that can think and act like human beings and incorporate thinking and acting accordingly.

Theoretically, the scope of Artificial Intelligence ranges from simple programs to systems that are more intelligent than humans. Many people believe that Artificial Intelligent machines will take over the civilized world, and just as many, perhaps more, think that is not true.

Machine Learning

There are two types of Artificial Intelligence: weak AI and strong AI. *Weak AI is* sometimes referred to as *Narrow AI,* since people like fancy names and also *Artificial Narrow Intelligence* (ANI), that are designed to perform specific small tasks. Some ANI systems are exceedingly simple like vacuum cleaners that can roan around the living room, and a little more complicated self-driving cars and IBM's Watson.

Strong AI is a group of AI's, including Artificial General Intelligence (AGI) or Artificial Super Intelligent (ASI) with intelligence equal to humans. It could do anything, such as solve problems and plan for the future. It would have super intelligence. Strong idea is a good idea, to some degree, but doesn't exist today.

This opens the door to deep learning and machine learning. Since the two names are used interchangeably, it is prudent to denote the difference between them. Machine learning is a sub

area of Artificial Intelligence, and deep learning is a sub area of machine learning.

The types of learning differ in how the algorithm learns. Non-deep learning uses human experts to analyze data while deep learning does it by itself.

Deep learning employs neural networks and is generally considered mor of what Artificial Intelligence should be. Neural networks is with Quantum Computing as two of the most complicated subject in advance computer technology.

Generative models take raw data and generate useful information. Generative models take raw data and generate useful information. Generate models are not new and are what the subject of statistics is designed to do. The modern Artificial Intelligence method use information to select data for display or other forms of computation.

Artificial Intelligence Applications

Most Artificial Intelligence writers summarize into 5 categories. They are: Speech Recognition, Customer Service, Computer Vision, Recommendation Engines, and Automated Stock Trading. Here is a brief summary of those categories.

Speech: Uses natural language processing to analyze human speech and generate it in a written form.

Customer: Called virtual agents that respond to customer queries, that may be questions, products, and sizes through customer engagement. Referred to as virtual agents or voice assistants.

Vision: Used to derive useful information from digital images and videos. Used in healthcare, law enforcement, or design by computer.

Recommendation: Use past consumption to discover data trends to improve various business goals.

Automated: Used to optimize stock portfolios and facilitate automated stock trading.

Cognitive Computing

Convention computing is, as practically everyone knows, is a pre-planned set of steps to provide a per-planned result. With convention, applications are conceived, designed, programmed or coded, tested, and then put into operation through a person-oriented scenario. The only intelligence is in the mind of the person's involved. The objectives are identified beforehand, and additionally, computing elements are designed to interact of a pre-defined manner.

With cognitive computing, elements are defined and combined to execute in an intelligent manner without human intervention. The computing elements may be defined and prepared or exist in the outside operational environment.

Machine Conversation

Machine conversation is a defined collection of natural language processing and machine learning elements. In its most simple form it is two conversational programs that talk to one another, such as ELIZA and ELIZA or DOCTOR and DOCTOR, mentioned previously in this report. Intelligent machine conversation involves two compatible intelligent entities interactions with one another.

Computer Speaking

The ability to initiate computer speech is a companion to speech recognition. It is usually combined with speech recognition and cognitive computing. A simple example is text reading and speaking. When combined with other cognitive elements, it is in the AI domain.

Empathy from Computers

There are two kinds of computer empathy: human empathy for computer technology and its various difficulties, and the empathy of computers to humans. Computer can sense emotion if defined beforehand. As yet, it has not been considered in the area of Artificial Intelligence.

Cognitive Systems

The discovery and understanding of unstructured information and cognitive sysems is generally combined under the title Generative Models.

A generative model is a deep learning facility that can take raw data, such as database information, speech, visual information, and other event data and draw relevant conclusions.

ChatGPT

ChatGPT stands for Generative Pre-trained Transformer. It's a complex computer system that generates text by responding to a user's input. It is a sophisticated and a well thought computer program in a software category known as Generative Artificial Intelligence (GAI). That's what some people think and others question the intelligent part and refer to it as generative software. It has received nationwide attention and more than 200 books have already been written on the subject. Some people love it and others think it will take over civilization, as people refer to it, and we will be extinct intellectually. By the way, that is called *Singularity.* You can go online to its developer, *OpenAI,* to use it. It's free and easy to use. The concept is popular, and you can even try an app for your iPhone that will also generate generative output. This information is given in this part of the book.

Introduction

ChatGPT is an Artificial Intelligence Chatbot_that uses natural language processing to create a human like conversational dialogue. The language model can respond to questions and compose various written content, such as articles, social media posts, essays, computer programs, and messages and emails.

ChatGPT employs natural language processing concepts, such as machine translation, information retrieval, sentiment analysis, and information extraction. Accordingly, ChatGPT is a form of generative AI wherein the user enters prompts and receives humanlike images, text, or video that are created with AI methods.

ChatGPT generates results that are similar to the automated output of customer service websites; the user asks questions or receives clarification of some sort and receives a response. With ChatGPT, and not necessarily with sister systems, the system uses the previous results to progress to the next level. As such, the ChatGPT system can create a scenario, written text, such as a novel, or conventional written material of practically any nature. Purportedly, ChatGPT can work with text, pictures, video, or any form of input.

During operation, ChatGPT uses internal scenarios to assist in generating appropriate results. The results may or may not be relevant to the intent of the user. Most users are enamored with ChatGPT results and there has been a distinct increase of persons

involved. For example, there are already more the 200 written and published books on the subject.

Using ChatGPT

ChatGPT uses algorithms to find patterns within data sequences by using language models named GPT-3 and GPT-4 and ordinary GPT. Information is not available on them. GPT stand for Generalized Pre-trained Transformer. You can run ChatGPT by entering:

https://chat.openai.com/blog/chatgpt

and you obtain a user ID and password. You are directed to facilities for using the ChatGPT program. Returning users need only to enter:

https://chat.openai.com

The information you enter is called a *prompt*. Follow the prompts and you are in. You are then directed to enter text and receive output from ChatGPT. A trial user is allows only 5 prompts per session and 50 per day. You can open a ChatGPT account for a $20 monthly fee and obtain a Premium ChatGPT subscription with access to other OpenAI models.

When you enter a prompt, ChatGPT yields a response computed with a complex neural network. The transformer generates a response and remembers the interaction that is used for the next prompt. Often the results are pure nonsense. Outputs are

not planned in any particular manner and often they not worth very much except for amusement. In a business environment, the outputs yielded by the transformer would make sense. There are probably organizations that are currently working on the use of ChatGPT to enhance their operational environment.

ChatGPT Internals

ChatGPT stores pattern of data entered my users and information systems and uses those patterns to develop its output. It uses neural network and probability to do its work. Each adaption of ChatGPT works in its own particular way based on its input. Each system uses a selected GT, that is Generative Transformer, to function and it used the database to which it is attached. As we are going to state in the conclusion, you can't just hire a summer student and expect an operational environment. The process will probably be similar to the original adoption of computers that used aas good set of operational systems and people who knew how to use it.

ChatGPT is not a search engine that takes input requests and thorough various mix and match operations, generates it output. ChatGPT takes input known and generates a response based on its stored patterns and the prompt. The work is performed by a selected transformer, such as two of them named GPT-3 and GPT-4, with varying amount of capacity and computational power. The transformers use a concept known as the *large language model* (LLM) to produce a natural language response to the prompt.

The key element in ChatGPT is a transformer that produces the responses through the use of a neural network of processing nodes similar in thought to the human brain. Neural networks are exceedingly complicated and perform the work of the transformer. Transformers have to be trained and different based on the data, such as test or video. There are differing methods of initiating a chat and responding to its output.

Social Aspects of ChatGPT

Whenever something new pops up, a groups of outsiders also pops up. Some of the areas are regulation, ethics of application, job loss, insurance, and so forth. There will probably some job enhancement opportunities and some decisions to be made by upper management. There will be no singularity.

The Author's Opinion

As with other areas of computer and information systems, some organization, such as IBM with computers and IBM, Oracle, Amazon, and Microsoft in database technology, some company has to step and take the lead. They have to come in and educate employees and install systems. It can't survive in generative artificial intelligence with shotgun advertising and hope for the best marketing. Direct marketing wherein sales people have a jurisdiction and go in and educate the potential customers is necessary. The fact that over two hundred books exist on ChatGPT doesn't mean much since many are independently published. A lot of people are interested in ChatGPT like they

were with computer games. ChatGPT is an excellent research area for universities and OpenAI must be a magnificent company. But, ChatGPT has a way to go. By the way, the first and best book on ChatGPT is Pam Baker's *ChatGPT for Dummies,* published by John Wiley and Sons, Hoboken, NJ, 2023. She assumes that you are 'smart and pressed for time and therefore want all meat and no fluff in a fast and easy read.'

IBM Watson

IBM Watson, usually referred to simply as Watson is a question answering system that can answer questions entered in common ordinary natural language. The Watson system first entered the world of technology in a competition on the Jeopardy! TV show against former champions. Watson won. I has since been evolved by IBM into a generative system for supporting end-user computing. Watson was a creative excellent wonderful imaginative project that only IBM could think up and execute with excellence. Watson is an effort that only a team with superior knowledge and fantastic management could pull off.

Introduction

Watson has since been adapted to an CLOUD service accessible to a myriad packages with generative intent. Now this is the author's projection or opinion, depending how you look at it. Then for each class of computer application, you need access and training packages for each application class, as well as user interface modules. This is what IBM has done with their

System/360 and System/370 computers to support through microprogramming several basic hardware models operate and be programmed as one computer design. Then, if you combine this with direct marketing, you have something to think about. IBM may already be doing that, how would I know.

Operational Considerations

In this form, Watson works in the same a manner as ChatGPT, and the end-user can look at it in that way. Of course, they are not the same. The user inters a prompt and the system does something. That something could be a an important business function or intended output of a visual or textual nature. During operation, the Watson system passes the prompt through a neural network system and generates an appropriate response. In so doing, it can be used to solve problems in the following areas:

- Coding computer programs.
- Composes music.
- Make wireless drafts of emails.
- Summarize articles.
- Writing social media posts.
- Creating articles.
- Making articles.
- Describing complex topics.

This is only a generic list that would be provided with any practically any generative AI systems.

Being an IBM product, Watson would probably avoid the following problems inherent with generative systems:

- Understanding the complexity of human language.
- Lack up-to-date information.
- Behave like a machine.
- Has poor analytics.
- Has trouble understanding the relevancy of specific data.

Watson would appear to be devoid of the given limitations, as stated.

How in Watson Works

The Most important feature of Watson is that it operates out of the IBM Cloud, which is an operational feature that is relevant to modern computer and data processing systems. All resources, except the user interface, reside and operate in the cloud and that is where all support modules and the Watson hardware and software reside. In order to use Watson, you have create an account that necessitates that you have to log in whenever you want to use your facilities. That is an application assistant that gives you the interface between your application and the Watson facilities.

You have to tell the application the *intents* which are the actions it will do for your application. Next, you have to identify *identities* that are the functions the assistants will do for you. As you can so, you are building an application interface. Next a *dialog*

has to be built in order for the end user can communicate with your application that runs on then cloud.

When you are dealing with vision, you have to build a *classifier*. So you can see how using the IBM Watson operates. It is deceptively simple to build an application and it is transparent to the user team.

There is a lot of literature on IBM Watson in advanced book form. It is no secret. The reference for the above information is: High, Rob and Tanmay Balshi, *Cognitive Computing with IBM Watson*, Birmingham: Packt, 2019. Rob High is an IBM Fellow.

Working with IBM

When dealing with a system that is being developed, the technological environment is pretty chaotic. Research people at various universities, scientists, professors, and students, along with capstone projects, theses, and dissertations in addition to the usual technological academic papers and reports. It's no wonder that there more than 200 books published on ChatGPT, many of which are independently published. *OpenAI,* the creator of ChatGPT, has done a miraculous job with their development

With IBM Watson, you have to buy into IBM, so to speak, and you are assisted in all phase of the project.

Index

Blogging 137

Boltzmann 24

Brain 4, 6, 9, 22–23, 25, 31–32, 49, 114, 176, 225, 236, 238, 240, 280, 282, 284, 299

Business agility 99, 101

Business-to-business 127

Business-to-consumer 127

C

Categories 87–88, 92, 116–117, 135, 140, 145–146, 158, 160, 164–166, 171, 175, 182–183, 186, 223, 265, 269, 292

Chatbot 261, 289, 296

ChatGPT viii, 261–263, 289–290, 295–301, 303

Chat room 132–134, 141

Classifier 303

Closed system 86

Cloud viii, 221–222, 300, 302–303, 310–311

CLOUD viii, 221–222, 300, 302–303, 310–311

Cognitive 2, 4–5, 7–8, 21–22, 234, 236–239, 265, 271–273, 278, 280–284, 293–295, 303

Cognitive computing 265, 271–272, 293–294, 303

Cognitive Science 2, 5, 7, 234, 237, 278, 281–282

Cognitive Technology 4, 7–8, 236, 238–239, 280, 283–284

Collaboration 95–96, 118, 122–123, 141–142, 161

Composite service 103

Computer Assisted Translation 15

Conceptual system 87

Connection Machine 4, 23, 25–26, 236, 280

Consumer-to-consumer 127, 136

Co-production 81, 155

D

Dartmouth College 3, 235, 279

Data Science viii, 226

Delegation 96

Deliver 103–104, 124, 128, 138

Descriptive 80, 88, 156, 179, 208

Diagnostic 217

DOCTOR 67, 69–72, 89–90, 105, 112, 169, 177, 180, 182–183, 258, 272, 294

E

Electronic data interchange 129

ELIZA 258, 263, 272, 294

Environment (of a system) 7, 29, 39, 47, 49, 85–87, 95, 107, 123–124, 126, 147, 160, 162, 167, 169, 183, 202, 226, 238, 272, 283, 293, 298, 303

Expert System 17, 28, 30, 32–37, 39, 41–42, 44–46, 49, 54–56, 58, 251–253, 265

F

Find 10, 39, 51, 120, 124, 128, 205, 211, 221, 241, 262, 285, 290, 297

Forward Chaining 38–40

Frozen middle 11, 242, 287

G

Generative viii, 223, 227, 261–262, 266, 269, 273, 289, 292, 295–296, 298–302

Generative AI viii, 223, 261–262, 266, 289, 296, 301

Generative Transform 289

Government-to-business 127

Government-to-consumer 127

Government-to-government 127

GPT-3 297–298

GPT-4 297–298

H

Hamming 232, 276

Handle 68, 95, 116, 133, 138, 266

Heterogeneous 78, 82, 182

I

IBM viii, 51, 65, 83, 108–109,
121–122, 141, 154, 187–189,
223, 226, 266, 268, 291,
299–303, 309

IBM Watson viii, 300, 303

ICT 97–101, 103, 111, 135

Identities 193, 210, 302

Information vii, 3–4, 10, 16, 19,
21, 24, 30–31, 34, 41, 44,
54, 57, 59, 63–64, 68–72,
75–76, 78–80, 82, 86,
91–92, 95, 97–99, 101–104,
106–109, 111–123, 125–141,
145–147, 149–154, 156–157,
172, 175–176, 178, 182,
188, 192–197, 199, 201–206,
208–210, 213–214, 216,
218–219, 222–223, 231,
235–236, 241, 243, 251,
253–254, 256, 258–262,
266, 269–270, 273, 275–
276, 279–280, 286, 288–
289, 292–293, 295–299,
302–303, 309

Information processing 3–4, 76,
118–119, 125–126, 136, 175,
178, 235, 279

Information service 64, 68, 91, 107,
111–117, 119–120, 122–123,
125–132, 134–141, 172, 176

Intangible 6, 67, 72, 80, 82, 89,
175–178, 184, 186, 238, 282

Intelligence vii, ix, xi, 1–7, 10, 13,
16, 25–28, 31, 43–45, 50–
54, 57, 115, 146, 158, 166,
205, 223, 226–227, 229,
231–238, 241, 244, 247–249,
254, 257–260, 263, 265,
267–269, 271, 273, 275–283,
286, 288, 290–296, 299,
310–311

Intents 296, 300, 302

Interaction service 120–121

Inventoried 79, 82

J

John Dewey 243, 259, 287

Joseph Weizenbaum 258

K

Knowledge Representation 7, 22,
28–32, 34, 47, 53, 108, 146,
154, 165, 188–189, 238,
248, 283

L

Large language model 223, 298

Learning 7, 29, 38, 49–50, 52–53,
224, 226, 243, 247–249, 259,
262–263, 265–269, 272–
273, 282, 288, 290–292,
294–295

LISP 47, 57, 253, 307

M

Machine Intelligence 52–53,
247–248

Machine translation 14–16, 44,
262, 289, 296

McCarthy 3–4, 235, 279

Middleware 121, 149, 153

Minsky 3, 235, 279

Model 3, 8–9, 22, 25, 31, 36, 56–
57, 73, 75, 87–88, 105–108,
112, 123–125, 138, 141, 146,
151–153, 156, 161, 163–165,
177, 189, 192, 223–225, 234,
239–240, 251–255, 261–262,
269, 273, 278, 284–285,
289, 292, 295–298, 301

Multiclient service 122

Multiservice 128

N

Natural Language 13–14, 16–23,
28, 34–35, 44–45, 53, 223,
248, 261–262, 269, 272,
289, 292, 294, 296, 298, 300

Natural System 13

Neural Network vii, 49–50, 56,
252, 262, 265, 269, 290,
292, 297–299, 301

Newell 4, 163, 188, 235, 279

Non-storable 73

About the Author

Harry Katzan, Jr. is a professor who has written several books and many papers on computers and other subjects. He has been an advisor to the executive board of a major bank and a developer on several major AI projects using LISP and Prolog. He and his wife have lived in Switzerland where he was an AI consultant and a visiting professor. He holds bachelors, masters, and doctorate degrees.

Books By Harry Katzan, Jr.

Computers and Information Systems

Advanced Programming
APL Programming and Computer Techniques
APL Users Guide
Computer Organization and the System/370
A PL/I Approach to Programming Languages
Introduction to Programming Languages
Operating Systems
Information Technology
Computer Data Security
Introduction to Computer Science
Computer Systems Organization and Programming
Computer Data Management and Database Technology
Systems Design and Documentation
The IBM 5100 Portable Computer
Fortran 77
The Standard Data Encryption Algorithm
Introduction to Distributed Data Processing
Distributed Information Systems
Invitation to Pascal
Invitation to Forth
Microcomputer Graphics and Programming Techniques

Invitation to Ada
Invitation to Ada and Ada Reference Manual
Invitation to Mapper
Operating Systems (2nd Edition)
Local Area Networks
Invitation to MVS (with D. Tharayil)
Introduction to computers and Data Processing
Privacy, Identity, and Cloud Computing
Advanced Technology and Essential Services
Cybersecurity as a Service.
Lessons in Artificial Intelligence
Artificial Intelligence: A Primer
Artificial Intelligence Concepts for Managers

Business and Management

Multinational Computer Systems
Office Automation
Management Support Systems
A Manager's Guide to Productivity, Quality
Circles, and Industrial Robots
Quality Circle Management
Service and Advanced Technology

Basic Research

Managing Uncertainty
Microprogramming Primer

A Tale of Discovery
The Terrorist Plot
An Untimely Situation
The Final Escape
Everything is Good
The Last Adventure
The Romeo Affair
Another Romeo Affair
With All My Love

Printed in the United States
by Baker & Taylor Publisher Services

Printed in the United States
by Baker & Taylor Publisher Services